Ethiopian Wildlands

Ethiopian Wildlands

Melvin Bolton

Foreword by Jeffery Boswall

Collins and Harvill Press
London, 1976

ISBN 0 00 262205 X
Set in Baskerville
Made and printed in Great Britain
by William Collins Sons & Co Ltd, Glasgow
for Collins, St. James's Place and
Harvill Press, 30A Pavilion Road,
London S.W.1.

To Hilary & Gavin

Contents

		page
	Foreword by Jeffery Boswall	11
	Introduction	15
1	Getting Started	19
2	South into the Rift Valley	31
3	The Plains of Nachisar	54
4	The South-West	75
5	Lake Stefanie	99
6	The Far West	114
7	On Foot to the Mago Valley	131
8	Ups and Downs in the North	144
9	Salt and Brimstone: the Danakil Depression	159
10	Nomads' Land	182
11	In Search of Beira	200
	Epilogue	212
	Index	217

Illustrations

MAPS	*page*
Map of Ethiopia	13
Map of South-West Ethiopia	17

COLOUR	*facing page*
Fish eagle	148
Yellow-billed stork	148
Black-headed weaver	148
Soemmering's gazelle	149
Beira antelope	149
The Simien Mountains	156
Simien fox	156
Nomad family and village boys in the Ogaden	157
The man from the salt caravan	157

BLACK AND WHITE

between pages 56 *and* 57

Soké boat on Lake Abaya

Jean Bolton at Lake Langano

Harrar girl basket weaver

Danakil girl filling goatskin water bag

Stones, mud and water – our Land-Rover had to cope with them all

Illustrations

between pages 88 *and* 89

Overlooking the Mago Valley

Orthodox priest

Danakil appreciates a cigarette

Hairdressing at a Danakil camp

between pages 136 *and* 137

Termite mound

Somali wild ass

Swayne's hartebeest

Greater kudu

Burchell's zebra

Beisa oryx

between pages 184 *and* 185

Hamlet in the Simien Mountains

Encounter on the way to Hammer Koké

The Danakil guide to Logia

The salt 'mine' at Dallol

Melvin Bolton on the salt flats of the Danakil Depression

Foreword

by Jeffery Boswall
Producer of the BBC television series
'Wildlife Safari to Ethiopia'

Melvin Bolton's eminently readable and well-informed book brought flooding back to me the delights and deflations, hopes and fears, joys and frustrations of travelling in that extraordinary country: Ethiopia. An African Tibet, Ethiopia is religious, rugged and remote. Bolton, lucky man, spent over five years there working as a wildlife ecologist and visiting the many and varied key areas for wildlife that Africa's least-known country offers.

Addis Ababa lies in the middle of a national triangle a thousand miles across its base, and another thousand from base to apex. Getting out of the capital whenever he could, the author followed most of the major points of the compass on one or another of his field trips.

He went north to the High Simien, a mountain massif offering some of the most dramatic scenery in Africa. Here live three of Ethiopia's four endemic mammals: the Simien fox, the gelada baboon and the walia ibex.

He went north-east into the baking Danakil Depression, home of the Somali wild ass, and due eastwards, first to the Awash National Park, then on to the Somali border in search of that rare quadruped, the beira antelope.

His achievement in penetrating the politically-troubled south-east of Ethiopia, the Ogaden area, is one that many people will envy him. There he found another strange and beautiful antelope, the dibatag or Clarke's gazelle, a little-known species.

Southwards from Addis, along a much-used route, lies the Ethiopian lake district, home to an impressive variety of birds; south too are the provinces of Arussi and Bale, the only known haunt of Ethiopia's fourth endemic mammal, the mountain nyala.

Some of Bolton's most enviable trips took him south-westwards to Lake Stefanie near the border with Kenya; here, on the baking flats of that seasonal lake, he found Grevy's zebra.

Finally, with Jean, his adventurous wife, Bolton went west to the swamps bordering the Baro River in the hope of finding 'Mrs Grey', the curiously-named lechwe of the Nile.

Having learned to adapt himself to the different climates and tongues of one of the most richly varied countries of the dark continent, and having explored it pretty thoroughly, Melvin Bolton in the book which records his journeys, effectively combines aesthetic appreciation, personal anecdote, scientific fact, and commonsense philosophy about conservation.

ETHIOPIA
SUDAN
ERITREA
Dahlac Islands
Massawa
ASMARA
Axum
Dallol Salt Plain
RED SEA
TIGRE
Takkazze River
BEGEMDER
Makelle
Lake Julietta
Assab
Simien Mts.
DANAKIL
GONDAR
WOLLO
Lake Tana
Lalibella
Logia
F.T.A.A.
DJIBOUTI
GULF OF ADEN
Bahar Dar
DESSIE
Bati
GOJJAM
Debre Marcos
Kembolcha
Awash River
Aysha
Blue Nile
Debre Berhan
DIRE DAWA
HARRAR
SOMALIA
WOLLEGA
SHOA
Awash
Chercher Mts.
Jig-jiga
ADDIS ABABA
HARRAR
Gambella
ILLUBABOR
ARUSSI
Degahabur
Awari
OGADEN
Lake Abiata
Fafan River
Lake Shalla
JIMMA
Galadi
Wardar
Shashamanne
KAFFA
Soddu
Omo River
Bale Mts.
Imi
Danan
Kebre Dahar
Arba Minch
Lake Abaya
Maji
GEMU GOFA
BALE
Godé
Kelafo
Webe Shebelle River
Lake Chamo
Mustayel
Ganale River
Lake Stefanie
SIDAMO
Moyale
Lake Rudolf
KENYA
Towns with over 30,000 inhabitants
Principal roads
Provincial boundaries
Approximate distributions of land above 5,000 ft
0 50 100 150 200 Miles
0 100 200 300 Kilometers

Introduction

'The successful candidate will be required to travel extensively and live mainly under canvas.' At the interview they had left me in no doubt about that. The one in pin-stripes had really stressed it. I had seen the job advertised under 'Overseas Appointments' in the leading newspapers as well as in the science journals. Applications had been invited for the post of Wildlife Biologist: Ethiopia. My application had needed no further soliciting, I'd got as far as the interview and would now be 'considered along with other candidates'. My final hope was that the others had made a worse mess of the interview than I had.

Africa had fascinated me since I was a boy. I had grown up reading of the magnificent mountains, rivers and awesome deserts of that great continent, trying to imagine it all and sometimes being defeated: the Sahara for instance – a desert the size of Australia. And all these wild places had their complement of beautiful and curious beasts which to my mind included some of the most exciting things possible. I suppose at one time I spent most of my school lunch-breaks digesting a bolted meal in the Natural History section of the public library, lost in a literary world of puff adders, plagues of locusts, gorillas, big cats, ostriches, okapis and numberless other creatures, many of them involved in sensational stories of the African bush which were probably nurtured on gin and tonic and should have been on the fiction shelves.

That was more than twenty years ago and my choice of reading, I later realised, was rarely in the best interests of my education, but it sustained my enthusiasm and I'd return reluctantly to school, through the north-country drizzle, with things to think about other than our rather dreary second-year syllabus in biology. The syllabuses became less dreary later on, which compensated for their getting a lot stiffer, and I had a hand in composing some myself eventually, for I came to teach biology for a time in England and abroad.

But when the advertisement from Ethiopia appeared, the most I had achieved on the continent of Africa was a little judicious shopping in Tangiers. On Ethiopia I hadn't even read very much, though I knew it possessed some very spectacular scenery and a few notable animals found nowhere else in the world. The fact that Ethiopia's remoter regions were so little-known, however, made the prospect of going there all the more attractive, positively exciting.

'What do you know about Ethiopia, Jean, apart from its once having been Abyssinia?'

'Not much,' she said after a moment's concentration. 'Capital's Addis Ababa, Emperor's Haile Selassie, there are mountains and historic churches.'

My wife knew no more than I did but she was quite willing to go there if we got the chance. At the library we agreed that our ignorance of the country and its fauna was excusable for we had trouble finding anything which had been written since the war that wasn't historical, political or antiquarian.

It was understandable that these subjects should dominate the literature in view of the chronology of Ethiopia's stormy political history. It all began, so the historians tell us, as long ago as 1,000 BC when the first colonists from South Arabia reached the Ethiopian highlands, which were at that time inhabited by purely Hamitic peoples – the dark-skinned indigenous folk of north-east Africa.

Still in pre-Christian times, these southern Arabs founded a kingdom whose capital was Axum in what is now the province of Tigre. Axum lay on an important trade route which stretched from the Red Sea, through Axum and on to the Nile. The Axumite kingdom flourished for hundreds of years and eventually became Christian but it began to decline after the seventh century when the Red Sea fell under Muslim control. By the tenth century AD the Axumite kingdom had collapsed and the city faded from the historic scene.

Violence and internal strife followed its decline but order was restored within a second Christian kingdom which was ruled by kings who had retained their Hamitic purity – the Zagwe dynasty. The Zagwe kingdom was centred further south, in present-day Wollo province where one of the Zagwe rulers, King Lalibella, inspired the construction of what are now Ethiopia's most remarkable antiquities, the monolithic churches of Lalibella. There are twelve of them in all; each hand-hewn from solid rock – and still in use as churches.

In the thirteenth century, following 300 years of rule, the Zagwe dynasty was overthrown by the Solomonic line whose kings trace their descent to Menelik I, legendary son of Solomon and the Queen of Sheba. Under the Solomonic kings the capital was brought to what was then the extreme south of the Empire – the modern province of Shoa. Christianity, and Ethiopian rule, continued to extend southwards but the newly-won territory was not held for long. In the sixteenth century Muslim invasions caused chaos which was aggravated by Galla incursions from the south.

Portuguese allies fought in defence of the Zagwe state. They succeeded, after an initial defeat, in killing the Muslim leader, Ahmed Gran. Ethiopia remained Christian but the power of the monarchy declined and the Empire fell into a state of disunity which prevailed until the last century when Menelik II came to power.

He was a remarkable man who regained territory which had been lost more than three hundred years before. He made conquests in the south and east which brought Ethiopia to its present shape on the map. He defeated the Italians at the battle of Adua in 1896 and founded and nurtured a new capital, Addis Ababa. Menelik died in 1913.

The history of Ethiopia then, is the success story of a mountain people with Arabian as well as African blood, who originated in the north and eventually came to rule the Empire from its central capital, Addis Ababa. Today the most powerful of the ruling highlanders, the Amhara tribe, make up about twenty per cent of the population though they are numerically dominant in only a small part of the great highland mass which rises like an island from the peripheral lowlands.

The lowlands, at least by Amhara standards, make up about half the country and this half, Jean and I discovered at the library, was the least documented; moreover it would be the lowlands where the successful candidate would be required to spend most of his time. That much we knew from the 'further details' supplied upon my response to the advertisement.

Ethiopia, and especially lowland Ethiopia, it appeared, still had its share of wild Africa's riches, but conservation measures were urgently needed if they were not to be lost forever. The Ethiopian government had become concerned about this and about the tourism potential which would be lost if the wildlife disappeared. No doubt the government was also aware that that year tourism, based on wildlife, had become the chief source of foreign exchange for neighbouring Kenya, outstripping coffee exports. Tourism in Ethiopia was still in an embryonic stage of development.

The government sought United Nations' advice, and advisory missions visited the country. Following their recommendations a Wildlife Conservation Department was set up and an Englishman, John Blower, was recruited from East Africa to advise on its operations. A first essential, John decided, was to find out what wildlife resources the country had left. He did a great deal of survey work himself during the first year and soon had three game wardens settled in proposed parks. But Ethiopia was not like East Africa. Communications in some parts hardly existed and its area is more than five times the size of Great Britain and more than twice that of Kenya. It was plain that years of full-time work would be needed just to complete the preliminary ecological surveys, but no trained biologists were available.

At John Blower's suggestion the Wildlife Department approached the British Ministry of Overseas Development for aid – this to include a biologist for survey work. Britain accepted the request and advertised the vacancy.

In due course a letter 'On Her Majesty's Service' brought the news that I'd got the job, and so it was that in October 1968 Jean and I found ourselves in Ethiopia with no fixed abode.

I

Getting Started

'I'm going to kill somebody, do you hear? I'm going to kill somebody and I'm not even going to care about it.' It was an American at the next section. His face was twitching and he had started to shout. We were in the customs office in Addis Ababa and my fellow-sufferer was not the first *farenge** I had seen cracking under the strain. I had been there every day for a fortnight, trying to extricate some equipment which was supposed to be duty-exempt. The American was attempting much the same feat but his stamina had been sapped by previous performances earlier in the year. This was my first encounter with Ethio-bureaucracy.

'Ato Bekele is not present,' said the man behind the desk. 'Maybe he will come if you wait.' I hadn't much choice. There were dozens of signatures to be collected and none of them, it seemed, could be obtained out of sequence. Until Ato Bekele had signed, the process was halted; no one could sign on his behalf. Outside, amid the traffic, a cow bellowed its discontent.

Addis Ababa, the 'New Flower' of Ethiopia, is a remarkably thorough mixture of wealth and poverty, splendour and squalor. Ultra-modern hotels, hospitals, offices and supermarkets stand within a stone's throw of the tiniest hovels with earth floors and no sanitation whatever. Everything stands among eucalyptus trees; they grow in rows and groves and coppices of sprouting building poles. A fine city centre is developing out of a tight collection of villages, it spreads in an urban-rural jumble for some thirty square miles.

In the central shopping areas there are swept pavements and pestering street boys who drive one to distraction. Elsewhere you walk in the road or pick your way along unmade verges. Little

* Name used to refer to white people.

blue Fiat taxis buzz about the streets in hundreds tooting at likely fares.

We walked around Addis a great deal in those first weeks, with hearts pounding in the thin mountain air. We walked between offices and up the long road to the British Embassy. It was warm and brilliantly sunny and the air had a special sort of clarity. We could smell the blue-green leaves of the eucalyptus and strange pungent odours of cooking. There were other odours too, best left undescribed. We passed little wayside markets where women sat beside handfuls of onions, garlic or peppers and spices. At water pumps the women gossiped as they filled their heavy earthenware chatties; old women and women looking old from hardship and childbirth, women in traditional white, calf-length dresses mingling with the first teenage girls in mini-skirts which barely covered their bottoms. Eight hundred thousand people live in the ninety-year-old city, and there are cattle, donkeys, sheep and goats. Above the rooftops wheeling black kites angle their tails and shine in the sun the colour of golden eagles. After dark, spotted hyaenas descend from the surrounding hills.

We talked and wondered about all this on our walks, just as we wondered about the tin can on a stick which served as an inn sign outside so many doorways and about why we so often saw men carrying bedsteads on their heads (we still wonder about that). Did the urchins chant '*farenge*' and 'money money' at every white face or could they tell we were newcomers? It was good in a way that there was so much to wonder at, for the waiting sessions were interminable. All the necessary equipment for my assignment had been sent from Britain. Tentage, camping paraphernalia, photographic equipment, scientific equipment, it was all there in bond. Some of it at the airport, some of it at the post office and the rest at the railway station. It would all need to be cleared item by item and the department it was consigned to had lost half the papers. Worse still, the most vital item of all, the Land-Rover, was still sailing the Red Sea.

At 5.45 p.m. (11.45 by the Ethiopian time-system in which day begins at dawn) the American went home. 'Soon we are closing,' said the man behind the desk. 'I don't think Ato Bekele will be coming now, it is better if you come back tomorrow.' So it went on.

Addis Ababa is served by three supply routes from the Red Sea; two Italian-built roads from Massawa and Assab and a railway built by the French from Djibouti in French Somaliland (now called the 'French territory of the Afar and Issa' but still often referred to as French Somaliland for short). The Land-Rover was expected to arrive at Assab which is Ethiopia's main port. Then there would be customs formalities. From Assab, so they said, it would be brought to Addis on a salt truck when one became available. It could take months and we hadn't got months to spare. I collected a pair of temporary number plates for the vehicle and bought two air tickets for Assab.

Assab is an old Arab town with a population of about 12,000. Today, although the Arab part of the town remains unchanged, there is a sprawl of newer buildings associated with the port. The airport managed to function without any buildings as far as we could make out as we bumped along the airstrip. All I could see through the rain was a sort of hangar without any roof. We stepped down on to the steaming runway and ran for it, along with everyone else who was destined for Assab. If the rainfall figures were anything to go by the town was getting its annual quota all in one day.

It was all very vague. No one spoke English and no one appeared to be in charge. There was a small waiting room and one or two huts inside the hangar and everyone congregated there. After a long time and a lot of shouting an airline official came scuttling in out of the rain. 'I'm sorry,' he said, noticing Jean and myself, 'we couldn't open the door of the baggage compartment, all the bags have gone to Aden.'

There are two hotels in Assab and we were taken to the older one by some well-meaning residents who gave us a lift from the airstrip. It was a comfortable enough place with a large hall of a dining room and huge ceiling fans which whirred above the tables. It had stopped raining by then and on the patio outside a gang of youths played western music on a juke box. Inside, the place was full of sailors, Russians by the sound of them, and a few Italian families. A couple of perspiring waiters were running between the tables and the serving-hatch where they bawled the orders to an Italian cook. Predictably, the fare was Italian. Our waiter spoke English. There was, he informed us, 'spaghetti with sauce of meat or sauce of tomato'; afterwards we could have 'veal of meat or veal of fish'. He grinned, wiped his nose on his napkin and flipped it back over his arm with a flourish. Jean closed her eyes.

The generator failed that night. The juke box went dead and all the lights went out. We drank wine on the patio by candle-light.

The following morning I contacted the Land-Rover agent whose name I had been given before I left Addis. He proved to be a charming man and his help was invaluable. The Land-Rover, he told me, was still on the ship, but at least the ship had docked and they would start discharging the cargo tomorrow. As soon as the Land-Rover had been off-loaded he would shepherd me through the labyrinth of red tape which would surround it. In the meantime, he suggested, why didn't we take it easy on the beach. We had brought our swimming things but as far as we knew they were now somewhere in Aden. When we got back to the hotel however we found our suitcase had arrived.

A description of the shore at Assab would read like a tourist brochure: golden sand, palm trees, warm blue sea and coral reefs. Not at all a bad place to have to waste a day or two. We strolled along the tideline past dark muscular bodies; some were playing with a beach-ball. I felt acutely conscious of thin legs which had not been untrousered in public for some time. They looked etiolated, like forced rhubarb.

There were rock-pools where we chose to swim, with big crabs and chunks of coral washed in from offshore reefs. Coral reefs are quite well developed further north, in the Dahlac Archipelago, where a marine park could be set up. With some facilities such as underwater observatories and glass-bottomed boats, anyone, from young children to old age pensioners, would be able to see the reefs and their brilliantly-coloured fish. There are no facilities, though. Instead there are reports that in the shallows the reefs are being destroyed by collectors. This is a great pity for even with future protection they will take many years to recover.

Coral colonies start from a tiny solitary larva which settles down and develops into a gelatinous polyp, like a sea anemone. The polyp divides repeatedly until a colony of thousands or hundreds of thousands of polyps is built up. Each secretes an external skeleton of calcium carbonate, limestone, which is all one usually finds when a broken piece of coral is picked up on the beach.

We fooled about among the rock-pools until evening and I had worked up a phenomenal appetite by the time we got back to the hotel. Faced with the same choice of food as the night before I opted for the 'veal of fish'. It tasted all right but perhaps it had been in the fridge during the time the electricity was off. Whatever the reason, I spent the next four days being violently sick.

Our agent friend collected Jean each morning and arranged for her to sign things on my behalf. Undoubtedly she made better progress in the customs offices than I could ever have done. By the weekend the Land-Rover was in a garage (which looked disturbingly like a scrap metal yard) being prepared for the drive back to Addis Ababa, while I was taking gentle strolls about the town trying to work up the strength to drive it. I met a man who lived beneath an inverted bathtub, I got to know some sleepy-eyed camels which lay tethered outside a store and I concluded one walk reflecting on the possible interpretations of an enormous notice on a wall which read 'NO URINE HERE'.

It is a little over five hundred miles to Addis from Assab, a two-day drive. You cross the Danakil Desert the first day and spend the second one climbing on to the western plateau and finishing the journey about 8,500 feet higher up than you started it.

About forty-five million years ago, according to some of the best authorities, the Horn of Africa and much of Arabia were raised up into a tremendous highland block. In Ethiopia the elevated mass of ancient rock was then capped by basalt and other lavas which erupted and continued to pour over the surface throughout the Oligocene, a period of some ten million years. There then followed the widespread fracturing of the earth's crust which has produced the existing rift valleys of Africa and the Middle East. Blocks of land hundreds of miles long have slipped down between parallel faults like huge sunken kerbstones. Precisely how the Rift System was formed is still a matter for dispute but very broadly speaking the rift valleys belong to three main units. There is the African Rift (here called the Main Ethiopian Rift) which divides the Ethiopian highlands into eastern and western plateaux and extends as far south as Mozambique, the Gulf of Aden and the Red Sea. These three units intersect in Ethiopia. The Danakil Desert lies in the intersection, in the fork of the Y which is called the Afar or Danakil Depression. Parts of it are below sea-level and were at one time below the sea.

Early visitors from Europe normally landed at one of the old Red Sea ports and in order to reach the Ethiopian highlands had to trek across the infernally hot desert by camel caravan. Today, the truck-drivers endeavour to avoid the heat of the day as far as possible by leaving Assab in the early hours. On Monday morning the lorries were revving and grinding past our hotel from about 3 a.m. onwards. Had I made the journey as often as some of those drivers I should probably have joined them on the road but we were keen to see the route by daylight and so we clung to our beds until dawn.

In the cool of the morning, with the sun rising behind us, we took in our first impressions of the Danakil landscape not just with interest but with awe. Upon the endless plains of open thornbush and sparse grass, dark stony seas of solidified froth stretched for miles. Elsewhere lava rubble littered much of the surface and the same blackish rock was strewn over the hills and ridges. It was basalt lava and in terms of the geological time-scale the big flows had been produced very recently, some of them within the last 200 years. The scrubby plants which find sustenance between the jagged rocks do little to soften the harshness of such a wilderness. There are many signs of active vulcanism in northern Afar. The crater of Erta Ale in the far north still holds molten lava. But even far away from the craters, the fumaroles and the main lava flows, the desert generally presents the same austere and inhospitable scene.

As one might imagine, the inhabitants of Afar are a tough lot and their reputation for ferocity had reached me through published accounts long before I arrived in Ethiopia. Most of the Afar Depression is occupied by people of several tribes calling themselves collectively the 'Afar' though others refer to them as the 'Danakil'. They have to a large degree remained purely Hamitic but like all the peoples of the eastern lowlands they embraced Mohammed's faith. The different groups are constantly at feud, especially with their Somali neighbours to the east, and they are said still to collect trophies from the victims of their many skirmishes. In my own experience, I'm glad to say, I always found them friendly, but I did take care not to upset anyone.

We passed numbers of these rangy nomads on the road; the girls naked above the waist except for ornaments and sometimes a black shawl, and the men, some with filed teeth and all with great curved knives slung in leather scabbards at their belts.

I noticed that the knives were invariably slung horizontally with the handle to the left and I remember wondering if all the Danakil were left-handed. When I came to work among them three years later I watched them draw their knives by passing the right hand across the body. It was explained to me that in this way, in case the knife is needed quickly as a weapon, it always comes to hand in a stabbing position. Not, I would have imagined, the best way to hold a knife in a fight but I'm sure the Danakil know best.

The Danakil are truly nomadic people, herding camels, goats, sheep and cattle in astonishing numbers. When a family is on the move their collapsible huts, made from woven grass mats and curved branches, are transported on camel-back; building material in the desert is much too scarce a commodity to be wasted. The erected huts are surrounded by a small thorn *zareba**. Only the little circular pens which protect the lambs and kids are built from stones. Those, and the tombs which rise, chimney-like, from the lava.

We saw only relatively common animals on our drive through the desert but most of them were new to us and we found it exciting enough. The snow-white hindquarters of Soemmering's gazelle fairly shone in the distant sunlight and drew attention to herds of these fawn-coloured animals which might otherwise have passed unnoticed. Some groups were quite close to the road and we could see clearly their black face-markings and lyre-shaped horns. Less numerous and much less conspicuous were smaller dorcas gazelles. We spotted only a few small groups and trios nervously trotting away with quick, springy steps, their little black tails twisting and wriggling like worms. If we slowed down and showed too much interest they would break into a run and could, I knew, maintain an incredible sprint for miles.

Desert antelopes as a group tend to be highly mobile, for where vegetation is sparse feeding must be spread over a wide area often without any cover from enemies. It follows too that they cannot range in the desert without spending a great deal of time far from water. A characteristic of desert animals is that they are able to manage for long periods without drinking. Some, like Soemmering's gazelle, can probably do without surface water altogether, making do with the moisture in the grass or leaves which they eat. When that fails they will turn to certain ever-green leaves and bush fruits which they normally disregard. They have their limits though and no gazelles can survive for more than a few days on an absolutely dry diet.

Desert birds as a rule need to drink regularly but ostriches, of which we saw fair numbers that morning, have an unusual tolerance of dehydration. Both the North African and Somali ostriches occur in Afar. The cock birds are easily distinguished, for the Somali type has a blue-grey neck and thighs instead of

* Protective enclosure.

the pink skin of the North and East African varieties. Seven feet tall, with striking black and white plumage, the Somali ostrich is a handsome bird. The male does much of the job of incubating the eggs, no mean feat, for ostriches are polygamous and several hens may lay eggs in a common nest, but during the day the dominant hen often takes a turn at incubating. For part of the time this amounts to keeping the eggs cool rather than warm. Up to sixty eggs have been recorded from single nests in East Africa. The Somali bird tends to have fewer eggs to cope with, perhaps because his harem is smaller.

We made slow progress from Assab, stopping frequently to scan the plains through binoculars, and the sun was far below the horizon before we reached Bati where we planned to spend the night. On every telegraph pole a large bird took perch just before dark. They were Egyptian vultures, white birds with bright yellow bills and particularly disgusting eating habits: nothing organic seems to be too nasty for them. I wondered where they went to roost before the advent of telegraph poles.

Bati lies among the foothills of the Western Plateau, a convenient stopping-place between the desert and the highland. It is also a well-placed trading centre for commodities such as grain, cloth or salt from the desert. Monday is market day in Bati and a steady stream of nomads and camels flowed past our headlights as we neared the village. There were rows of parked trucks when we got there and only one small hotel, but as most of the drivers were sleeping in the cabs we had no trouble getting a room.

Next morning we had barely started when we were stopped by a ragged individual who thrust a pudding basin through the open window of the Land-Rover. We had slowed down to crawling speed in order to edge around a crater in the road when the pudding basin, wrapped in a filthy rag, was dumped in Jean's lap. She looked at me enquiringly.

'What do you make of this?' she asked.

'Christmas present, might be a Christmas pudding if you're lucky.'

Jean was not amused. The ragged fellow now had his head through the window in his efforts to explain things and kept pointing down the road. I suppose we were a bit slow to catch on but it eventually dawned on us that we were being asked to deliver it to someone further on.

It was a *wott* pot; a bowl of the hot, pungent stew which is the daily fare of the Amhara people. In Addis we had caught wind of it many times but never actually been introduced to it. As I breathed the fumes from the present dish I decided we hadn't missed much but I was wrong, we came to be fond of *wott*. Cheap *wott* or the fast-time variety can be made from beans or lentils but the more extravagant dishes may contain mutton, beef or chicken and hard-boiled eggs. In each case the strongly-flavoured liquid part of the stew is very hot with red peppers. *Wott* is invariably eaten with *injera*, which feels damp, tastes sour and looks like grey or brown circular sheets of foam rubber about a quarter of an inch thick and two feet or so in diameter. It is made from the partially fermented batter of ground teff (*Eragrostis teff*), a small-seeded grain plant which is one of Ethiopia's major crops. You tear off pieces of *injera* with which to gather up mouthfuls of *wott* – and the combination goes down surprisingly well.

It was no problem to recognise the rightful owner of our little cargo. He was standing, straw hatted and in calf-length, patched-up jodhpurs staring disconsolately at yet another large hole in the road. Obviously the road menders had been distributed by lorry early in the morning and this poor chap had become separated from his packed lunch. He also seemed to have come without any tools. His eyes lit up when he saw the familiar food bundle and a grin split through the black stubble of whiskers.

'This yours?'

'*Ishi, ishi,*' bows and more grins. '*Egzerstilin, egzerstilin.*' We left him, still looking rather helpless, but not quite so forlorn.

The gravel road wound on through green, steep-sided valleys with dwellings and cultivation wherever the slopes permitted settlement. The roads from Massawa and Assab converge at Kembolcha, a well-appointed little town at about 6,000 feet.

We stopped there for a beer and sat watching the combined traffic from the north and east rumbling on towards Addis Ababa; it didn't amount to very much.

We were in fact sitting where we could keep an eye on the Land-Rover. It was the open, pick-up type (later to be converted to a lock-up hard top) and the canvas and other bits of equipment were lying factory-wrapped in the back. It wasn't long before three curious-looking characters began to show more than a casual interest in our vehicle but they certainly didn't look like dealers in stolen car parts. One wore long robes, not the usual toga-like *shamma* of the highlanders, and had shoulder-length ringlets of greasy hair with a sort of turban on top. The other two were only slightly less strange and looked just as unwashed. Each clutched sticks and horse-tail fly whisks. They were wandering preachers, and with a sequence of bowing and an intoned chorus of pleading they gradually made it known to us that what they wanted was a lift to Addis Ababa. In addition to the legions of Orthodox clergy in Ethiopia there are thousands of such parish less priests. They receive no stipend from the Ethiopian Orthodox Church (often still called the Coptic Church though the last ties with Alexandria were broken in 1958) and depend entirely upon alms for subsistence.

With the clerical hitch-hikers safely in the back we left Kembolcha and continued southwards towards the ascent of the plateau. Beyond the village of Debre Sina the escarpment, which is the western wall of the rift valley, looked almost vertical and it was quite unthinkable that there could be a road ahead. In parts the road had indeed been blasted out of the vertical rock face. At the entrance to a long tunnel the name MUSSOLINI was clearly legible in the stonework above although there had been some attempt to obliterate it with cement. One got the impression that the Italians must have devoted the whole five years of their occupation to building roads. We passed through the tunnel and Afar was lost from view.

We were now at an altitude of about 10,000 feet and it was drizzling and bitterly cold. The sodden shacks of the tiny roadside communities offered little comfort and our passengers, huddled together behind us, waved us to go on whenever we glanced enquiringly through the rear window. At Debre Berhan, the last town before the capital, they climbed out and, thanking us profusely for their eight-hour ride, limped off to find lodgings. The petrol pump attendant smiled and said something which, as usual, we didn't understand.

2

South into the Rift Valley

It is more than a hundred years since the first National Park was established; that was Yellowstone in Wyoming USA, set up in 1872 to preserve for public enjoyment the scenic wonders which so thrilled the first European explorers.

Today there are over 1,200 parks and reserves throughout the world, which being adequately protected and administered, qualify for inclusion in the UN list of National Parks and Equivalent Reserves.

There are a few nations which need no special justification for devoting large tracts of land to nature conservation, but much more often, and increasingly so, wildlife and wild places have to pay their way in competition with other forms of land use in a crowded world. Agriculture, multi-purpose development schemes, irrigation schemes, dams, roads and the sheer pressure of multiplying people needing somewhere to live, force even the most enlightened governments to think twice before adopting conservation policies.

The problem is most acute in underdeveloped countries where arguments based on sophisticated concepts such as amenity value, aesthetics, education, long-term benefits of research, and responsibility to future generations, are incomprehensible or even insane to a predominantly illiterate populace of hungry peasants. Politicians who advocate giving land and money to wild animals and plants under these circumstances are not likely to be appreciated.

Fortunately during recent years a solid economic case for conservation has revealed itself in underdeveloped countries: tourism is a lucrative industry. Visitors from the crowded west pay a small fortune to see and experience what the local peasant farmer is not yet able to appreciate. So one can hope that money from tourism will continue to provide the incentive for conservation policies, at least until less mercenary motives become viable. In setting up a national scheme of parks and reserves attention must therefore be given to those areas where tourism is a feasible proposition. A profitable tourist industry can also subsidise and help to justify conservation in those areas which are inaccessible, or for some other reason too difficult to develop for tourists for the time being.

Naturally enough, the most accessible parts of Ethiopia were the most well-known and the best road of all ran south into the Rift Valley. The previous missions to Ethiopia had already made provisional recommendations to set up a park there, among the Rift Valley lakes. It was a good place to start work, so after preliminary discussions with John Blower, we left Addis on the road south.

The Main Ethiopian Rift runs north-north-east from the Kenya border, bisecting the highlands before funnelling out into Afar. Within this great rift valley, a million years ago, huge lakes formed and later shrank to produce a chain of smaller ones, each of which has now acquired its own special characteristics. About 130 miles south of Addis Ababa four of these lakes, once confluent, now lie in a cluster. Lake Zwai is fresh and fringed with reeds, Langano is brackish, deep and rugged. Abiata is also salty but shallow and gently shelving, while Shalla is 800 feet deep, a fifth as salty as sea water and scenically magnificent.

The road south runs as a straight dual carriageway through the outskirts of Addis, often as congested as a market-place. It was to become our most familiar road out of town. I recall very well the first time we travelled it; later one ceases to take notice of familiar things. We passed big petrol depots, grocers' shops, bars, embassies, residencies and night clubs with names like 'The Buffalo Club', 'The Romance' and 'Shanghai' crudely painted on home-made signboards with arrows pointing into a chaos of tin-roofed buildings.

'Not all that good,' an Ethiopian once remarked, 'the girls are all worn out.'

Beyond the town the land was a patchwork of unfenced fields, some under ripening barley, others studded with low haystacks for it was December and the harvest was in progress. Across the fields distant mountains formed an indistinct and indeterminate wall though the sky was blue and the air was brilliantly clear. On the right, and not so far from the road, an isolated volcano, Mount Zuquala, rose 2,000 feet above the plains. There is a church at the top and a shallow crater lake which some hold sacred. It was a good tarmac road and steadily downhill all the time. For some reason the rift wall doesn't exist in this region and the road and rail dip gently from plateau to valley bottom. There is a string of untidy villages along the way with starving dogs, Coca Cola signs and people driving donkeys. More often than not they leave the road at the sound of a vehicle – the people that is. The donkeys, left to their own devices, do their best to run into the car. Occasionally a bus comes whizzing along with a blaring, yodelling siren of a horn and loudspeaker music. Then everything gets out of the way.

After an hour or two Galla people began to dominate the villages, folk with darker skins and broader features. The Hamitic Galla tribes, Ethiopia's biggest ethnic group, make up about forty per cent of the population. Addis Ababa is surrounded by predominantly Galla communities and there has consequently been a great deal of intermarriage with the Amhara people; tribal distinctions in the capital are by no means easy to make. Three hours' drive away from Addis, however, they were Galla of the Arussi tribe, assertive inhabitants of the mountains to the east and that section of the rift. There had been a village market and the women were wearing their finery; engraved brass bracelets, beaded head-dresses and pendent necklaces of glass beads; swinging splashes of colour looking particularly striking against their dark skin. They wore capes of goat or calf skin scalloped at the edges and fringed with the same glass beads. The pelts are kept supple with butter which the girls also rub into their own skin so the olfactory effect, though strong, is unattractive. The men wore assorted garb, most were in shorts and a *shamma*. They often carried a spear or stick across their shoulders with both arms draped over it in a crucifix position, a habit one sees all over Ethiopia. We were passing through open acacia woodland where men lounged in the shade beside stacks of charcoal. Three dollars a sack, they were asking, two fifty if you brought your own sack. Truckloads of it arrive in Addis where thousands of tiny braziers cook *wott* and *injera* and all the local charcoal timber has long since gone.

According to old hunting records the woodland used to teem with big game but the only animals we could see beneath the flat-topped acacia trees were goats and cows, thousands of degenerate cows, grazing and nosing almost at the grass roots. It was painfully clear that much had changed in Ethiopia during the past few decades. Range management experts calculate that this part of the Rift Valley is now five times overstocked with cattle. The dry, stubbled ground was engraved with a fine network of dusty cow tracks converging at favoured crossing points on the main road. One scrawny herd issued on to the road in front of us, ambling across to water at Lake Zwai. A herd boy, stick across his shoulders, trailed after them with a cursory glance at the Land-Rover; cars always managed to stop in time, it seemed.

To the left of the road we caught tantalising glimpses of Lake Zwai shining through the trees. Abiata was further south, on the other side of the road. The Wildlife Department had already established a small game-guards' post there and we had decided to make our first base-camp nearby. A bridge marked the turning and our track followed a little river, the Horacallo, which flowed into Abiata from Lake Langano. We passed a sort of bay where we later watched chestnut-bellied sand-grouse coming in thousands to drink. Each morning the flocks would come sweeping into view like plump, khaki-coloured pigeons on long, pointed wings. At precisely the same time thousands upon thousands of sand-grouse would rendezvous at this little bay which offered a nice smooth approach to the water but was too small for more than a few hundred birds to be at the water's edge at once. They crowded into the bay and the first row of drinkers would hurriedly fill their crops. As they flew off the next in line would already be waddling forward to take their place. With exemplary orderliness legions of thirsty birds watered at the same place and dispersed again in a matter of minutes. Such are the habits of sand-grouse wherever they occur.

We arrived too late in the day to see them that first morning. They had been and gone. Above the little bay a lone pied kingfisher hovered on rapid wings, sighting down its long vertical bill. It looked like a cartoonist's impression of a giant biting insect. On the track in front of us two enormous marabou storks strode slowly and solemnly along the bank. Side by side and walking in step, hunched forward with their black wing tips meeting behind, they looked from the rear like two elderly gentlemen in dress suits or a couple of ageing professors in academic gowns. There was a sense of killing time rather than purposeful progression in that slow, measured step, as if at any moment one of them would produce a gold watch from a waistcoat pocket and they would start strolling back to where they had come from. Instead, they took flight as the Land-Rover approached, spreading their eight-foot wings to reveal great gangling legs and galloping along until they became airborne. There were fish eagles and a tawny eagle perched in the trees while below them, unconcerned, sacred ibis jabbed at the turf with their long curved bills. I screwed a longer lens on to the camera; this was bird-watching of a rare order.

At the lake itself the birdlife was nothing less than astonishing. We stopped to take it all in through binoculars. Offshore, great white pelicans were fishing communally, moving forward like a line of beaters, sometimes encircling the fish they were driving, before all submerging their cavernous bills together. White-necked cormorants nested in hundreds on drowned trees and dumpy little grebes dived for tiddlers and bounced on the surface like bathtub toys. In the shallows thousands of lesser flamingoes formed huge drifts of pink as they skimmed the mud with their upside-down beaks. The waterline was patrolled by ruffs, sandpipers, little stints and wagtails while spur-wing plovers swooped and scolded us from above. It being the northern winter the resident African birds were sharing the lake with thousands of Palaeoarctic migrants. Every niche seemed overcrowded. In the space of a few minutes we had counted fifty species.

'*Tenastilin!*' The greeting came from two game-guards. They had appeared from nowhere and were standing trying to look polite but obviously curious about the two new *farenges* who had the department's insignia on their Land-Rover door. I introduced myself with a letter from head office and after muttering through it for a few moments they started jabbering and gesticulating with a vigour which was exhausting to watch. They kept it up for a surprisingly long time before realising that they were not communicating. One of them then branched out into dumb show. It was an involved little act which concluded with the resourceful guard leaping on to an imaginary bicycle and riding round in tight circles, legs pedalling furiously and arms extended to hold the handlebars. The other guard looked on approvingly. I couldn't make head or tail of it, and Jean was equally at a loss. The poor fellow eventually gave up and, very uncharitably, we thereafter referred to him as 'The Loony'. His companion was a stocky little figure who kept his face, especially his nose, screwed up in a sort of silent chuckle. But it was an honest, friendly expression, not that annoying 'private joke' sort of look. We took a liking to him and he became known from the decoration in his hatband as 'Flamingo Feathers'. We never discovered what the pantomime was about.

From inside the Land-Rover the two guards directed us to their outpost on the shore of the lake. We drove at some distance from the water, on firm ground where the acacias began to peter out. Closer to the lake only a creeping grass grew on the damp flats where a thick crust of pumice gravel floated over soft black mud. It was no place for motor cars. At the water's edge a thin tideline of white crystalline substance sparkled in the sun. It was a residue of sodium carbonate, a sort of natural washing soda from the lake. In the water itself the flamingoes formed their own band of colour, a moving ribbon of pink.

There were two other guards at the outpost and a full complement of wives and children. It was a square *chika* (mud) house with a corrugated iron roof and walls of mud and straw plastered on to a latticework of eucalyptus poles; not unlike the wattle and daub of mediaeval England, and surprisingly durable. Since sheet metal roofs appeared on the scene this type of house has become most popular in Ethiopia, springing up wherever there are permanent settlements and people who can afford the corrugated sheet. In contrast, about half a mile away there was a Galla settlement where the huts were all of the traditional circular *tukul* type with low conical roofs of thatch.

Having been introduced to the other guards and families, and shaken hands all round, we selected a spot and set to unpacking and assembling the camping gear which had taken more than two months to wring from the customs offices. Despite the well-meant but rather unskilled assistance from the guards it didn't take long and we were soon squelching along the waterline to see some more of the birds.

Abiata is fed by two small perennial rivers: the Horacallo, and the Bulbulla which brings fresh water from Lake Zwai. The two rivers are not far apart and the guards' post was situated between the two. Before long we found ourselves at the mouth of the Bulbulla, a region of swamps and pools where the river merges with the lake. We picked our way along stretches of firmer ground. In the dappled shade of the acacia trees, *Crotalaria* bushes were hung with racemes of yellow flowers and mint-scented *Tagetes* plants grew thickly beneath huge fig trees at the water's edge. Provided you didn't stir up the mud, which was indisputably malodorous, it was all very lovely. We were in fact in the richest corner of the whole lake. Nowhere else were we to find so many habitats represented in such a small area as that little estuary; a few green acres between the soda lake and the dry savanna.

The birdlife was incredible, everywhere one looked there were birds; frog-eating birds, fig-eating birds, birds of more than forty different families; hundreds of species, thousands of birds, most of them feeding and many of them noisy. On the open water the dabbling and splashing of ducks never ceased; mainly they were shovelers, sifting plankton from the water with their spatulate bills. The flamingoes kept up a steady cacophony of honking and raucous muttering, and starlings held a chorus of whistles and squeaks. Against the background commotion one heard the soloists; the cry of a snipe whirling over the rushes, the wild, ringing laughter of fish eagles or a goliath heron flying ponderously and croaking like a gargantuan frog.

Later, when we had some estimate of the numbers involved, I worked out that for much of the year the fish-eating birds of Abiata could not be existing on less than 25 tons of fish a day, excluding the weight of fish-fry which was being eaten by the sifting feeders. It is usually reckoned that a growing animal uses only about one-tenth of its food intake for body-building; the rest is wasted or burnt up in merely keeping the animal alive. The actual figure varies with different kinds of animals but ten per cent will do as an average and a rough rule of thumb. Twenty-five tons of young fish would have had to consume something in the order of 250 tons of plant plankton if they had been feeding exclusively as vegetarians. In fact, the fish include small animals in their diet which adds another link to the food chain, possibly two links since some of the small animals which get eaten may also have been carnivorous. With only ten per cent of the food intake being passed on at each link in the chain, it follows that the initial weight of plant plankton would be far in excess of 250 tons. All this was being removed every day from eighty square miles of water by the fish-eating birds alone. In addition there were some 10,000 lesser flamingoes feeding directly on microscopic plants and more than that number of ducks eating mixed animal and plant plankton; not to mention the waders.

It was one of those paradoxical situations where the animals appeared to grossly outweigh their food supply and yet obviously continued to flourish, like a swarm of locusts living forever on one potted plant. But no natural laws were being broken, or even stretched. There was just a rapid rate of turnover. In a healthy tropical lake the standing crop of plant plankton is continually reproducing itself as fast as it is being eaten and in Lake Abiata that was very fast indeed. The lake was a self-perpetuating soup.

Shallow tropical lakes are characteristically highly productive, which is why half the people of the world survive by eating swamp-grass products grown in home-made swamps. But Abiata was doing better than any rice paddy and there might even be fanatical production biologists who would see the lake from that point of view, as a sort of intensive food production unit. Such a production man would have no use for binoculars; his would be instruments of measurement and his note-book would be filled with figures and calculations of profound significance. 'Available solar energy,' it might say, 'so and so million calories a day. Plant plankton, so and so many tons a day (he would have this worked out in terms of energy too), animal produce (wasteful) so and so tons a day.'

'Think of it,' he would exclaim, 'thousands of tons of fresh nourishing plant life going to waste here every week. If only we could harvest it and serve it up as a palatable plankton-cake it could feed a whole town. Of course the diet would have to contain an adequate proportion of protein but then these micro-organisms can produce protein four thousand times faster than cows can produce meat. We could include fish in the system too, provided they were vegetarians, but we must find an effective pest control scheme to keep these wretched birds down.'

I have never actually heard of anyone quite as rabid as this. But one does read this sort of thing, quite seriously written, to the effect that there is no problem and all will be well for the future provided we use the food resources more and more efficiently and stop thinking in terms of free-range eggs and using good productive land for Sunday picnics. This preoccupation with food supplies, however optimistic, strikes me as being rather sinister in itself, for it suggests that the world has already given up hope of anything more in life than having enough to eat. As an aspiration for humanity it would seem more appropriate to a colony of underfed rabbits.

Evenings are short in the tropics and the lake was gleaming red as we made our way along the shore back to camp. Cormorants were homing in to roost from all points on the lake, and in the trees, birds squabbled for perching space. A small brown eagle, probably a booted eagle, flew low over the water, frightening the flamingoes into a sea of fluttering crimson. We turned and followed his course westwards into the lambent sky. Lonely and aloof, he remained apparently unaffected by the panic which raged a few feet below.

There were a few camp chores to attend to when we got back and the last of the daylight went all too quickly. Soon it was quite dark. We brought the gas cooker inside, zipped the mosquito netting across the front of the tent, lit the lamp and prepared to cook the first hot meal of the day. It was cosy and just pleasantly warm. Outside, the water lapped gently upon the shore and from far off came the monotonous thumping of a witch doctor's drum. It was a calm night and the few drops of rain which started to patter upon the flysheet mattered not at all. Jean busied herself with sizzling pans and I began to scribble some notes.

I suppose it was about half an hour later that Jean pointed and stared, horrified, at a shapeless mass of brown jelly which came oozing through a gap at the bottom of the mosquito netting.

'What on earth is that?'

I peered at it in the lamplight and prodded it with a fork. It disintegrated into smaller clumps, each seething like a bran-tub full of maggots. On a dark night it is impossible to see through a mosquito net when you are on the same side as the light. Inside the tent, with the noise of cooking and the hissing of the gas mantle, we had not seen or heard anything of what was happening. Lake flies, attracted by the only light on the shore, had settled in millions on the tent. Layer upon layer of midges moistened by the rain, had turned into a sticky jelly of dead and dying insects. On the vertical mosquito net the jelly had slid down and begun to ooze in at the bottom. On the sloping flysheet, as we discovered in the morning, it had merely continued to build up in thickness. My first reaction was to go out and inspect the mess and I started to unzip the net without even having the wits to hold my breath. I zipped it up again, hastily, coughing and choking in a cloud of tiny, whining insects which surged past me into the tent. Obviously the only way to stop the siege was to put out the lamp. We ate our fly-peppered supper by the faint light of a torch with a cloth over it. After cleaning-up operations next day we learned from the game-guards that the flies were being unusually troublesome; presumably a combination of suitable weather for the adults and the right conditions in the lake for the developing larvae. Our Abiata work was completed under a wartime blackout regime.

There were other problems too, on that feathered lake. Like most of the lakes in the Rift Valley, Abiata is subject to squalls which blow up very suddenly from complete calm. We were caught out by them more than once but the first time was the worst. It had been a day of boating, circumnavigating the lake in a little aluminium dinghy with a lawn-mower of an outboard engine. We had been collecting data on birds and lakeside vegetation and were on the home straight when a breeze began to stir. In no time at all the lake was reminiscent of the North Sea and we were holding ourselves in the boat with one hand and baling phrenetically with the other. I had forgotten to put the baling can in the boat that morning and we had to expel what seemed like half the lake with the top of a Thermos flask and a tennis shoe. Somehow we stayed afloat and even got the boat to go part of the time in a homeward direction. After four hours of it, soaking wet, blinded by salt spray and numb with cold, we reckoned we ought to be within sight of the guards' house but by then it was so dark that we could scarcely see the land. Because of the lake flies and the absence of glass in the windows, the guards' house was shuttered and showed no light. I became convinced that we had passed the spot and were pitching our way round the lake for the second time. When I could stand the thought no longer I gave up the struggle and waited to be thrown ashore.

We landed in fact about three miles short of the target. At least we recognised where we were and in which direction to start walking but I managed to lead us both into an agonising patch of thornbush before reaching the Land-Rover which was parked near the guards' place. We had moved our camp a few days before to a fenced compound some distance away where the fly situation was not so bad. When we got there it was to find that the tent had been raided by dogs. The homeless curs had torn the mosquito netting, eaten our cheese, bread and bacon, crunched up the plastic egg boxes and dribbled raw egg all over the sleeping-bags. The very next day we moved camp to Lake Shalla.

Shalla is a beautiful lake, separated from Abiata by a range of low hills dominated by Mount Fiké, 1,500 feet above the lakes. From the top of Fiké one can look down into a great rock basin where cliffs plunge vertically into the water and a small group of craggy islands rises almost as steeply from the depths. It is a lake of more than a hundred square miles, blue and shimmering through the sunlit calm but dark and violent through the storms. Here and there hot springs bubble from the rocks and send steaming rivulets into the lake. One small but permanent river flows from the rift wall on the east side, bringing fresh water to Shalla throughout the year. But there is no outlet and so, by evaporation, the lake has become salty and alkaline, exceptionally so for such a deep lake. It is what the limnologists would call an oligotrophic lake, a water of little food. Fish are plentiful only near the river inlet and there are relatively few shallows to support marginal vegetation or feed water birds. It is a deep and noble lake and birds which gorge themselves in the sun-warmed shallows of Abiata come to nest on Shalla in comparative peace and security.

We had trouble finding peace and security. The camp had to be located on a stretch of flat ground reasonably close to the fresh water inlet but the locals also favoured this part for grazing and watering their innumerable cows. They were not the sort of people to smile politely and walk past and we had them with us in a troublesome sort of way from dawn till dark. Eventually I dismissed the camp guard, whom I had only recently acquired and don't remember very much about, and brought Flamingo Feathers from Abiata. He was very tactful and good at keeping people away. He would engage them in conversation at a distance and could keep it up, if he had to, all day. Judging from the glances we got I suspect his technique was to say scandalous things about us and pretend that he could only divulge such confidences if we were out of earshot.

We moved, after a few days, to another spot about half a mile away. I found it quite by chance, a little secret glade among the lakeside bushes. We moored the boat out of sight, tucked the Land-Rover away and came and went like burglars. It took the locals all of forty-eight hours to discover where we were. Had there been a few more clumps of bush to investigate it would have taken them longer. But most of the shore, though not without trees, was cleared of undergrowth to provide more grass for the cattle. It was cropped to a low turf which after dark was astir with the shuffling and scraping of dung beetles.

They were everywhere; black, solidly-built creatures an inch or more long, struggling and pushing at their balls of dung. They walk on their 'hands' as it were, and push with their rearmost pair of legs, not always to mutual advantage when two or more beetles are propelling the same ball. The idea of the game is to get the ball underground as a food store or a repository for the female's egg. In the latter case she pats and smoothes the ball into a perfect sphere with a little space all around it. The egg duly hatches into a grub which eats away the dung from the inside until only a shell remains. The grub then pupates and a month later a dung beetle emerges in search of dung from which to shape a new ball.

It was interesting, at night, to prowl around the cow pastures with a torch. There were porcupines and civets, and a thing called a zorilla, related to weasels but looking like a miniature skunk. In the pre-dawn we saw hyaenas. They were about, of course, all night but only in the half-hour or so before sunrise did we see them. They ran in packs of up to half a dozen, a habit which is common in some parts of Africa but which I never saw elsewhere in Ethiopia. Several had dens near our camp and we would be awakened at about 5 a.m. by their whooping and howling. I tried to get pictures on high-speed black and white film but the light was never good enough; by the time it was, the hyaenas had gone. They were all the spotted type and would first appear as vague shadowy forms moving with a characteristic lolloping gait. I discovered that I could attract them by lying on my back and waving my legs in the air. They would move in with throaty noises, craning their thick necks and sniffing. But I never got pictures . . .

The river which flows into Shalla does so through a forested valley which lies cupped between the curving cliffs and the lake-shore. It is a very small and not particularly exciting forest as African forests go. The undergrowth was a scratching tangle and the trees, at that time, were not doing anything interesting botanically; most displayed an undistinguished foliage of quite unidentifiable leaves. But there were some fine *Podocarpus* trees along the river and the forest was home for a number of creatures, including at least one pair of leopard, which were not to be found elsewhere around the lakes. They were secretive and successfully so. Only once did we see a leopard, standing on the track to our camp one night, about a mile from the forest. He shone palely, eyes gleaming in the headlights for a few moments before he vanished into the shadows.

Occasionally, judging from the remains we found, the leopard managed to catch the colobus monkeys on the infrequent occasions that they descended to the ground. The colobus were plentiful in the Shalla forest, as indeed they are in most Ethiopian forests, despite the tens of thousands which end up as rugs in Addis Ababa. They are conspicuous monkeys too, and a pleasure to watch. Families would move through the canopy and a succession of black and white bodies, tails streaming like white plumes, would hurl themselves across the gaps and plunge into the slender and violently-swaying branches of the other side. It was not only beautiful and entertaining to watch, it was an exhibition of supreme skill in judging distances. Having both eyes at the front has made such precision possible in man and monkeys. Binocular vision evolved in the trees and colobus monkeys have perfected its use there.

At sunrise the colobus could be seen only from above, in our case, from the cliffs. The dark green canopy of tree-tops would be flecked with white as the colobus troops stretched and warmed and scratched themselves in the early sun. When this ritual was over they would disappear into the foliage to breakfast upon leaves and buds. It is not a very nourishing diet so they need a lot of it. In order to cope with it all, they have a large sacculated stomach and a conspicuous pot belly – a feature evidently not incompatible with agility.

The Shalla forest had at one time been continuous with a wide belt of forest stretching from the lake-shore, across the floor of the rift and high up into the eastern highlands. Clearance of forest by cultivators had isolated the Shalla forest as a remnant. There was still good cover on the slopes of the rift wall, though, which as the Arussi Mountains, rose steeply from lake level to over 12,000 feet. Flamingo Feathers and I trekked up there during the lakes survey, with four pack mules. It was an exhilarating if rather unfruitful exercise which took us through seven days and as many different zones of vegetation, from lake-side pastures to the forest of giant heath which grew above the tree-line. The forest proper was a tall, dark stand of fine timber trees where brambles and bracken ferns grew in the clearings and mosses covered the fallen logs with a soft deep velvet. Were it not for the colobus monkeys which crashed and rustled above and the outlandish cawing of hornbills one could have imagined one-self to be in an English woodland. The forest of trees gave way, sporadically, to brakes of mountain bamboo where progress was difficult and this in turn opened out into a delightful sort of parkland where *Hagenia* trees, looking slightly like horse-chestnut, scattered autumn-tinted leaves upon the damp grass. Progress here came almost to a complete stop for we were confronted by an armed band of horsemen who ordered us back. The boy in charge of the mules spoke a little English, and through him, I believe I told them what terrible repercussions there would be if they interfered with us. I then strode on trying to look unconcerned. Nobody shot me and the rest of my tiny expedition came following on. I felt very brave for the rest of that day and I like to think the incident did something for my image; Flamingo Feathers looked mildly impressed.

It was the same day that we came upon an old Galla grave with an outstanding example of stone sculpture. The gravestone showed a mounted spearman and some of the animals he hunted, including elephant, though the last Arussi elephants were wiped out by ivory hunters around the turn of the century, using guns, not spears.

The giant heath was rather disappointing when we got there. Mostly it stood about knee-high and the country resembled a grouse-moor rather than a forest. The locals burn it regularly to improve grazing for their cattle. A few patches of forest did remain to show what the mountain tops used to look like at that altitude. The gnarled and twisted heath trees, fifteen or twenty feet high, grew close and were festooned with masses of grey-green lichens. It was still and silent there and the mist lingered. Tramping in the gloom beneath the dripping canopy I found the effect eerie. But the glades were spangled with wild flowers and the silvery leaves of lady's mantle (*Alchemilla*). There were everlasting flowers in white and yellow and the flame-coloured spikes of red-hot pokers (*Kniphofia*) grew in scattered clusters. At its lower limits the heath was mingled with the *Hagenia* trees and yellow-flowering bushes of St John's wort.

We looked, unsuccessfully, for mountain nyala and visited the place where, a few years before, the distinguished naturalist Leslie Brown had seen a herd of nine. Mountain nyala are unique to Ethiopia and were only made known to science as recently as 1908. Weighing up to 500 pounds the male is a huge brown or grey-brown antelope with spiral horns like its relative the kudu, though with less turns of the spiral. Nyala usually run in small herds, yet the bulls are often solitary. They still occur in the Arussi Mountains but there is too much burning and destruction of their habitat and their main stronghold is further south in the mountains of Bale where you might see two dozen in a day. Bale is beautiful country, like the very best parts of the high Arussis. A National Park was proposed there following Leslie Brown's surveys of 1965, but it still hasn't been gazetted.

National Park status was very evidently what was needed for part of the Rift Valley and it had by this time become apparent that it should be confined to the immediate vicinity of Abiata and Shalla. When we got back to Lake Shalla we found that Jean, who had been having a week's rest, had experienced a revival of enthusiasm for boating. On the strength of it she had organised the transfer of our aluminium dinghy from Abiata to

Lake Shalla. Offshore at the camp site it bobbed and tugged gently at its painter as if impatient to be off.

The boat trips on Shalla were without incident, apart from a flaying dose of sunburn. We were cautious to the point of being faint-hearted for Shalla went berserk during storms and we did not really believe, not implicitly, that two expanded polystyrene camera boxes stuffed into a pair of Jean's tights were as good as any other life-belt if the boat capsized during a storm in the middle of Shalla. The boat was a boon, for to walk to the other side of Shalla took two days but we could boat across in a couple of hours. And the boat was the best position from which to examine the steep faces of the cliffs. Klipspringer found ideal habitat there and their tiny pointed hooves would thump away their positions as they bounded up the grassy but near-vertical slopes like thickset mountain goats. Twice we saw one standing on the limb of a fig tree which hung out over the water. It ran down the inclining tree trunk with no more trouble than a cat. We treasured the boat; without it we could not have got to the islands where the bird colonies nested. Admittedly we already knew what was there, for two ornithologists had studied the colonies in detail during previous years. But to see the birds for ourselves was a treat not to be missed, and we stopped off at each of the islands in turn.

One of them was little more than a huge wedge of rock protruding from the water. Stunted trees grew in the crevices and they were crowded with sacred ibis, white-necked cormorants, and Abdim's storks with blue and crimson faces. They all sat about, panting in the heat and evidently feeling secure for they displayed a bored lack of interest in the couple of raw-nosed humans who crept and crawled about their breeding isle to spy on them. Not so the pelicans, theirs was a busy community on another island. There were several thousand pairs of pelicans and only one favoured nesting place which they used on a rota system throughout the year, but with a peak nesting-period from December through March. The eggs take a month to hatch and the young spend another nine or ten weeks becoming fully-fledged. It had been found that at the age of about a month the half-fledged youngsters collect in crèches and move away from the nesting sites which are then occupied by another batch of egg layers. The whole cycle was in full swing when first we stepped ashore on Pelican Island.

The breeding area was a flat shelf of rock conveniently overlooked by a ridge. We could go chugging quietly up to the island on the blind side, drag the boat ashore in a hollow and walk up the ridge without being seen. We walked at a crouch, unnecessarily, like people who pass beneath helicopter blades which are whirring away two yards above their heads. We feared that the birds would be easily alarmed and I was frankly terrified of raising a whole colony of panic-stricken pelicans. If this were to happen I would feel like the poor devil who realises that he is clapping and stamping at the end of the First Movement. Actually the consequences of upsetting the pelicans could be serious. Many birds will readily desert their eggs from fright, though they become much more reluctant to do so around hatching time and thereafter as the parental drive increases. But we didn't know, until we saw the colony, that the breeding peak was tailing off and most of the parents had fledglings. It was a remarkable sight; great white pelicans are white, but the fledglings, hundreds of them gathered in small flocks, were chocolate brown with black bills. They looked like baby pterodactyls or the reptilian ancestors of birds, rather than young pelicans. Scattered among them were the parent birds, looking huge, as indeed they are. Other adults were soaring high about Mount Fiké like giant gulls. One by one they would come planing down to the island and waddle up to the crèches. A monstrous bill would open like a chute and a fledgling would plunge its head inside and gulp away hungrily. Each pair appeared to have only a single youngster though it had been discovered that, more often than not, two eggs were laid. There were no nests to speak of, just a scrape in the sand or a few sticks gathered together on the bare rock.

We stayed for hours on top of the ridge, watching the comings and goings of one of the biggest colonies of pelicans in Africa. From an observation point of view it could scarcely have been more convenient. We did not disturb a single bird apart from a hole-nesting duck, a Cape wigeon, which came bursting out of a burrow at Jean's feet. As far as the local folk were concerned the islands of Shalla were as secure as they possibly could be. The islands were too small to support habitation, there was no drinking water, and there were no fish. The greatest threat came from uncontrolled recreational activities. On Lake Langano, just a few miles away, people would be playing transistors and tearing about on water skis. The hotel would be full of weekend holiday-makers. A good thing too, Langano was the place to go for that sort of thing, but a few of those holiday-makers on Shalla would be the end of the bird colonies and of Shalla's special and rather dignified appeal. I don't believe that I ever saw a situation which had such potential for a multi-purpose land-use scheme. With proper zoning of activities in space and time it could be an out-standing example of how to make the most of things, but without planning and control it would all come to nothing in a sorry sequence of lost opportunities.

The lakes survey took four months in all and that was followed by a lengthy period of policy discussion in Addis Ababa. It must have been about six months later that the park plans were approved and a legal man was sent from the Wildlife Depart-ment headquarters. He, an Amhara, would negotiate with the local governor and the Galla chiefs, explain about the park and show them where the boundary was to run. But first he himself had to be shown what was involved. John Blower was in Addis at that time and was only too pleased to join us on the boundary demonstration. He was a keen field man and a walk around the lakes promised to be a pleasurable exercise and a welcome break from the office. It didn't quite work out that way.

The trouble was that we found ourselves, in the hottest part of the year, marching steadfastly into the next few days with hardly any water. We never really understood how it happened; both of us carried a small ex-army water bottle on our belts, indeed I had come to feel quite undressed without one, but each of us seemed to have been under the impression that the other had loaded a bigger water bag on to the mules. It was only when we wanted to fill it up at the first river that we found there was nothing to fill.

'But I thought you'd packed it,' we both protested.

Later, I knew, we would cross a seasonal stream which usually had a few pools throughout the year. We ought to reach it the following day and if we could hold out until then we would surely meet a Galla who would sell us a large gourd or clay chattie. If the worst came to the worst (and it did) we could walk more or less non-stop each day and make do with the bottles on our belts for the whole trip. The rest of the company were all Ethiopian and didn't seem unduly perturbed at the thought of having no water.

It was a long day, with repeated delays while the muleteers adjusted the loads. We also had to make wide detours to get the mules through the little forest of Shalla and it was late afternoon by the time we emerged on to the southern rim of the Shalla crater. There it was fairly clear going and with a superb view of the lake. We collected the inevitable gang of hangers on, ever hopeful of extracting a dollar from a naïve *farenge*, but mostly they only followed for an hour or so then dropped out and were replaced by others. The few we asked about gourds were miles from their homes and had none to spare anyway. We gave up; the conversations took too long.

One or two of our followers were unusually tenacious. There was a Muslim called Ahmed who stayed with us for the whole circuit, and a very odd-looking character (he never gave his name and religion, in fact he never spoke at all) who singled me out and lurched along behind me, leering, for most of the afternoon and part of the next day. I found it disturbing: he looked completely mad. He had a grubby *shamma* wrapped around his head and clutched a vicious-looking billhook at waist-level, as if he intended to carve out my kidneys. Shouting at him had no effect. He seemed content to walk a few yards behind, for though I kept turning round quickly, I never caught him closing in. All the same I kept an ear finely tuned to the clumping of his sawn-off Wellington boots. The mules at this time were far behind, for the pack animals were tired and the spare mules were being ridden.

John marched solidly in front, a big man, straight, and faintly military. He stopped at one point, mopped his brow with his bush hat and squinted into the sky. An airliner droned somewhere out of sight. John waved an arm helplessly.

'Think of it,' he called. 'Air hostesses and iced lagers.'

I grinned at him. He wiped a bristly moustache with the back of his hand and strode on.

On the south side of Shalla the land falls away from the crater edge down to settled, fertile plains. We walked along the crater lip which was a dry ridge of land where locals came only to cut acacia wood and graze goats. We were still several hundred feet above Lake Shalla when night fell, warm and clear. We set up our camp beds and prepared to sleep under the stars for there was no need to put up the tents. With water it would have been perfect. We felt parched.

'Just how salty is Shalla?' asked John. I told him. 'Well, is it possible to drink it?'

I said you could if you held your nose, but I didn't think it would do us any good.

'At least we could gargle with it,' John persisted.

Flamingo Feathers was with us and he volunteered to find a way down the moonlit cliffs and bring up some lake water in a billy-can. His stamina was impressive. He was gone for ages and when he finally staggered back the gargle and mouth-wash were not really worth it, at least not to me. John looked philosophical. 'I suspect', he said, 'that your friend Sweeney Todd will sneak up on us in the night and cut all our throats.'

He evidently found the prospect of swift decapitation preferable to the thought of dying of thirst, for he promptly fell asleep. He left me feeling worried. I thought no one had noticed my little problem. Where was he, anyway? He'd still been around when we were putting up the beds. Fortunately I was too tired to spend all night feeling uneasy.

While the mules were being loaded next morning, we tried

ultra-strong coffee as a way of imbibing Lake Shalla but still it couldn't be done. The next source of water was a hot spring. Half a day's walk is really very little but over difficult terrain with a lot of gasping and panting under tropical sun I need to drink about a pint an hour – more if it's available. We set off to an early start, anxious to cover as much ground as possible in the cool of the morning. Sweeney Todd appeared from wherever he had spent the night and it was a relief to find that he distributed his attentions rather more fairly than on the day before. We struggled on through the acacias, crashing in and out of gulleys to follow the boundary-lines where necessary and stopping now and then to point out landmarks and boundary beacon positions to the company. By the afternoon it was an effort to swallow and I was having hallucinations, foaming beer-mugs to be more explicit. We reached the hot springs by about 3 p.m., drank like camels at the sulphurous water and pressed on to reach more water by nightfall.

We had come down off the cliff-tops and were marching between the waterside and an unwalkable ridge of hills which was to form the western boundary. It was a hot, dusty haul. The earth was white with crystallised salts from the lake and the Galla were scraping it into heaps to be later carted off as salt-licks for cattle.

We stayed that night by a tiny pool in a seasonal water-course. There were cows there when we arrived and two Galla women splashing their faces and washing their hands. We filled the water bottles, dropped in a couple of chlorine tablets and prepared to wait the age-long thirty minutes for them to take effect. John looked anguished.

'Can you assure me,' he croaked, 'that these ladies never wash below the waist.'

'I don't believe they do,' I said.

'Thank goodness,' he breathed, and drank his fill.

The other thing about being short of water, of course, is that you have to walk further each day than you would normally choose to do. Feet seem to be able to stand just so many hours of battering in every twenty-four; stay within the limit and you can walk indefinitely, exceed it and things start to go wrong. By the end of the third day I had awful blisters and I remember John muttering something about the sole having come off his foot.

After four days we arrived, hobbling, at the appointed rendezvous with Jean and the Land-Rover. Over gallons of scalding tea we discussed the possibilities and contingencies of the future park. We talked about boundaries and the past four days. We had not, of course, been in any real trouble; merely, as John laconically put it, *in extremis*.

3

The Plains of Nachisar

In 1966 the Sandhurst Royal Military Academy launched an expedition to the Lake Chamo and Abaya area of Ethiopia. It was a training exercise mainly, but they took civilian scientists along as well as military specialists and they carried out a survey which included wildlife. The subsequent report tells how the team navigated a crocodile-infested river with Land-Rovers lashed on to specially designed rafts and how they struggled for days to winch the vehicles through mud and water. It also tells how they discovered large herds of game animals when they got to the other side of the lakes. All this took place shortly after John Blower arrived in Ethiopia. He visited the place himself and decided that it should be looked at more closely in order to properly assess its possibilities as a reserve and to select appropriate boundaries. It became our second safari.

Driving down the lakes road from Addis one reaches, after 150 miles, Shashamanne; a town which an American acquaintance once referred to as 'Ethiopia's other armpit'. It is hardly a spa town but it lies within a few miles of Mount Abarro, a forested ridge on the eastern wall of the rift. Up there, among the *Podocarpus* trees and the wild date palms, there are thermal swimming pools and a weekend retreat at that time used by members of the imperial family. Mountain nyala slip quietly across the clearings and melt away through the bracken and brambles. They come down, in places, to the foot of the mountain, less than 6,500 feet above sea-level and surely the lowest part of their range.

I have happy memories of Mount Abarro. The discomforts and irritations of hours spent in a tree-hide have faded and only the highlights remain; the sound of footfalls on dead leaves, a rustling of branches and the slow, thrilling appearance of a bull nyala in the viewfinder.

We escaped from the squalor of Shashamanne along an all-weather road which leads west through populous farmlands to Soddu, a small town on the top of a hill where it seems always to be either damp or raining. Thatched *tukuls* nestled like clusters of mushrooms in the shade of eucalyptus stands and false bananas. Women carried water and stooped over pots, men worked in the fields and, with their sons, herded stock. The way-side scene was typical of settled Galla or Amhara country. Yet most of the people were neither, for south-west Ethiopia is inhabited by many groups collectively referred to by outsiders as the Sidama. Though they are not Galla-speaking their languages are of the same family as Galla, Cushitic, and they merge with their Galla neighbours on almost all sides except the western borders where they mingle with a complex of more negroid tribes with Nilotic affinities.

At Soddu we stopped for a snack at a small hotel at the top of the hill. There were thick-billed ravens there which had become tame; they had learned to perch close by, making peculiar growling noises and soliciting tit-bits. They are all-black birds with a white nape patch and a heavy, curiously expanded bill.

The petrol station is next door to the hotel, a fact to be noted with satisfaction for it saves one the bother of having to go into the main street past the usual uninviting row of shacks which serve as bars, shops and everything else and which are invariably infested with followers and pesterers.

With a full tank we continued down the Rift Valley and into drier country to the west of Lake Abaya. We could see the lake before we got down to it, a huge brown, reedy stretch of water with islands ranging from bare rock to sizeable portions of land which had huts and permanent residents. At one point the road ran just above the lakeshore for a while and we saw a group of the island-dwellers punting across the still water on what looked like a papyrus boat with a high prow. At closer range it obviously wasn't papyrus nor was it being punted exactly, but it was not until a year or so later that I fully satisfied my curiosity about those boats. They are made from a waterside tree which the locals call *soké* (*Aeschynomene elaphroxylon*). The wood is lighter than balsa wood and has a soft, fibrous texture. Whole trunks of *soké* about fifteen feet long and tapering from a diameter of perhaps nine inches at the base are laid side by side and pegged together with foot-long splints of bamboo. A series of V-shaped cuts nicely judged on the upper side of the trunks permits the ends to be bent upwards in the sweeping curve of the prow. The punting poles each have a block of *soké* fixed to the end, like an enormous bottle cork on the end of a stick. The boat gets propelled usually by two punters at the rear pushing against the buoyancy of the corks. It works extremely well, at least when the islanders do it. The boats last about three months, after which they become waterlogged and have to be replaced.

We stopped at Arba Minch, the capital of Gemu Gofa province. The hotel there is situated so that from its balcony you have an excellent view of both lakes. Well, part of both lakes, for Chamo is a good twenty miles long and Abaya is twice that length.

Directly below, between the lakes, a broad valley dips to water level then climbs steeply on the far side to continue as a high causeway running east-west and separating Lake Abaya from its sister, Chamo. *Ye Egzer dildi* (God's Bridge) they call it in Amharic.

From the hotel balcony, the following morning, we considered our next move. We planned to spend a couple of weeks or so at the other side of the lakes. To cover the area it would be necessary to move camp each day and for this we would require transport. Somehow we would have to get donkeys or mules across God's Bridge. We looked down on to the dense canopy of forest in the valleys below. It was riverine and groundwater forest and from the extra-tall fig trees and waterside acacias we could follow the course of the Collofu River. It flowed out of Lake Abaya, was swelled by the main river flowing from the hills behind us, and continued southwards into Lake Chamo. It was this river barrier which had given the Sandhurst team so much trouble three years before.

Soké boat on Lake Abaya

Jean Bolton at Lake Langano

Harrar girl basket weaver

Danakil girl filling goatskin water bag

Stones, mud and water – our Land-Rover had to cope with them all

For reasons of logistics we had kept the company to a minimum, one inscrutable game-guard called Berhanu, Jean and myself. After breakfast Berhanu marched off to find out about pack animals while Jean and I went to the Governor's office to present our letter of introduction from the Wildlife Department. It was a formality which I was to come to regard as one of the standard tests of my diminishing reserves of patience.

On this occasion it wasn't too bad. We sat for an easily tolerated length of time in a secretary's office and amused ourselves by watching the secretary, an elderly, bespectacled and terribly solemn gentleman. He tapped upon an old Olivetti with two fingers and repeatedly shuffled and reshuffled heaps of dog-eared files as if to doubly brief himself on the most momentous affairs of state before committing his final decisions to writing. He was typing some memo about road construction.

The Governor, like all provincial governors, dwelt in a big office below the requisite portrait of the Emperor. He had an interest in wildlife and liked the idea of National Parks. He ordered his exalted secretary to prepare a letter there and then which would ensure our unimpeded passage beyond the next police post. On the question of pack animals he was not able to be so helpful. They were a scarce commodity in Arba Minch. But we were to come and see him again if we had no luck.

As Berhanu found out, a local policeman had a virtual monopoly of mules for hire so it was lucky that his animals were unusually well cared for. We came to a reasonable agreement for two of them. I had been able to borrow some imported pack saddlery for the survey so loading up next morning was no problem except for the unavoidable gathering of watchers and 'helpers'. In no time at all, after the mules arrived, we were threading our way through the shady Collofu Valley. Lianas hung in loops from the greenery above and the early sun came slanting down in narrow shafts, sparkling on the beads of moisture which everywhere clung to spiders' threads. The cool air was laden with the scent of damp, forest earth.

It was down there, below the hotel, that the 'forty springs' issued with trout stream clarity from the base of the cliff. The local youths took a special delight in drinking from the cupped leaf of a waterside plant which is covered with a fine pile, like velvet. It had the effect of trapping a layer of air under the water so that it shone like a silvered mirror. It looked more like mercury than water. I never counted the springs or '*minch*' but '*arba*' means forty.

One of these quicksilver boys showed us the best place to attempt the river crossing. We emerged from the forest at a place where the river had divided into two deep channels. A flimsy bridge of branches and lianas had been slung across the first and major channel and a slightly more rigid structure spanned the second one. For people there was no problem but with loaded mules the river was a serious obstacle. As we stood and looked, two huge Nile crocodiles launched themselves silently into the coffee-coloured water.

It took most of the day to build up the bridges, using logs and branches and levelling off the surface with bundles of rushes. I was anxious to get the crossing over that day even if we only set up our camp on the opposite bank. The mules had been relieved of their loads before we started bridge-building and it was decided to lead them across unloaded and make several journeys ourselves to carry all the equipment. We brought up the first mule just as a party of locals arrived to watch the entertainment.

Our mule took one look at the steeply-sloping tree trunk which led on to the ridiculous catwalk across the river and refused to budge. We gave the other one a try. The guide who had helped all afternoon led him to the brink. There was a moment's hesitation, a dreadful slithering of hooves and he was clumping steadily across the bridge. We had the second mule close behind; he still refused to budge. We wheedled and coaxed, tried him with different leaders, covered his head, whacked his backside, all to no effect. Our audience joined in enthusiastically with their own techniques but none of it did any good. We set up camp in the fading light while the guide rode the mule back to Arba Minch.

By 8.30 next morning we had a replacement and the crossings

went without a hitch. We followed a stony track over the saw-toothed range of God's Bridge and the following day we left the far shore of Lake Abaya and toiled in a crush of cows up a narrow defile to the Nachisar plains.

Like the lakes further north, Abaya and Chamo were at one time confluent and the Nachisar plains must have formed a huge shelf on the floor of the ancient lake. The plains now lie several hundred feet above the eastern shores of the lakes and they extend eastwards in a series of hills and undulations for several miles before descending to the foot of the Amaro Mountains which once formed the eastern limit of the combined lakes and now present a scenic backcloth to the grassland.

The word Nachisar is an anglicised version of *nach sar* which is Amharic for white grass and refers to the light colour of the grasses there which are dry and dead above ground for much of the year. Early in the wet seasons the plains are as lush and green as an English meadow. It was the end of August, the beginning of the late rains. There had been a storm during the night and the sticky black clay of the old lake bed clung to our boots in great clods as we lugged our feet eastwards towards the Amaro range. It was worth the effort to outpace the cattle and their attendant swarms of flies. The cowherd was a boy of about twelve whose face was insensitive to flies; he did not even blink when they crawled across his eyeballs.

A little herd of Grant's gazelle watched us suspiciously and a group of Burchell's zebra stopped grazing and looked up, uneasy, as we trudged past. There were no other wild animals in sight for although there are nearly 300 square miles of plains, there is so much undulation that it isn't possible to see far except from the highest parts. Here and there accumulations of clay and straw looked like birds' nests, each with a deep hoof print in the middle; evidently the zebras sometimes found the sticky clay as troublesome as we did. On the higher ground and in extensive patches elsewhere, the surface consisted of an ankle-twisting jumble of lava boulders half hidden in the grass. It was unpleasant going and Jean began to lag behind, due to blisters. The three of us plodded on, too far apart for conversation and not in any case having much to talk about.

Gradually the day brightened up. The clouds of the damp and dismal morning cleared away and the sun came to raise our spirits. In the late afternoon we clattered down a scree slope from the plains into the shady valley of a stream. It was the Sermale. It flows along the foot of the Amaro range, collects an outflow from Lake Chamo, and continues down the rift as the Sagan River. It made an idyllic camp site, despite a few tsetse flies. We pushed up the tents beneath the acacias while the mules, freed from their loads, rolled and snorted in the dust.

While Jean rested and Berhanu guarded the camp I spent the next few days exploring the Sermale Valley and mapping from the Amaro foothills. It was pleasant and peaceful. I wondered what it was like beyond the mountains away to the east, for at that time I had not seen the green, rolling hills of Sidamo province. It is excellent farming land there, with coffee plantations on rich loam which had formed under forest trees.

The Amaro foothills were much lower and drier and had probably never been heavily forested. Now the steep slopes were quite open, with a cover of grass tussocks and scattered shrubs and bushes. Mountain reedbuck would lie out in full view but I never saw them until they had seen me. There would be a shrill alarm call and two or three small brown antelopes would go bounding off with flashes of white from their upturned tails. In dense cover by the stream there were shaggy-coated defassa waterbuck, big, chunky animals with fine ringed horns in the male. Their coat colour varies in different parts of Africa but the Ethiopian specimens were always a rich reddish-brown with blackish lower limbs. They used to leave the thickets in the evenings and graze where we could watch them, if the wind was right.

I met few people and the ones I did meet were content to exchange a greeting and go their way. Some came from hamlets far up the mountainside. On one day I didn't see a soul, an uncommon experience in Ethiopia for the twenty-eight million inhabitants seem to be distributed just about everywhere. In the highlands it can be difficult to spend an uninterrupted half-hour, let alone a whole day. At Nachisar the few resident pastoralists tended to keep their *tukuls* fairly close to the lakes though they made full use of the plains for grazing stock.

We were reluctant to leave our camp in the valley but there was a lot to be done and because of the amount of food we could carry, days were strictly limited. So move we must, back across the plains to the Chamo outflow, then on to a series of points along the shores of the lakes.

The earth was dry now and the going was easier. Berhanu drew ahead leading one mule, the other following close behind. He was a stoical character, a thin man with a prominent jaw. He walked stiffly with his feet, as they say, at ten to two. He never spoke much and hardly ever ate as far as I could see but as long as he had his cigarettes he was contented enough and a willing assistant. Jean and I fell behind, constantly stopping to look at things or collect grasses for the plant press. Little piles of grass seeds, now dry and fluffy, lay where the harvester ants had gathered them. Quail burst from the ground on buzzing wings and vanished again into the grass a few yards away. A secretary bird ran with loping strides, disturbed in its quest for grasshoppers and perhaps an occasional snake which it would kill by stamping on it. As it ran the plumes behind its head wagged rhythmically up and down; they earned it its name. Presumably someone decided they resembled quills behind the ear of some Dickensian clerk. Also searching for grasshoppers, and anything else small enough to be caught and eaten, were three pairs of Abyssinian ground hornbills, big, heavy black birds with monstrous bills and a casque like a sawn-off tube on top. They have no feathers on the face and throat, just bare skin, red in the males, blue in the females. The nearest pair took to ponderous flight as we came too close, swishing their broad wings to show startling white patches.

But even in dry weather, walking across the open grassland could never be very enjoyable. Tripping and stumbling over the lava boulders is irksome enough, though with practice it gets easier, but to add to the discomfort the grass was crawling with ixodid ticks whose tiny imperceptible bites later itch unbearably.

Clusters of newly-hatched larvae clung to the grass in brown blobs which brushed off against our legs and slowly exploded into thousands of minute ticks which disappeared into our clothing.

Dragonflies, the hawks of the insect world, were in constant attendance and these at least were agreeable companions. They flew in swarms around our legs, hovering and darting with incredible precision as they preyed upon the smaller insects flushed from the grass by our blundering feet. I tried tossing a few ticks in the air but I don't think they got eaten. On level ground you can side-step the more conspicuous tick blobs provided you see them in time, but on lava it isn't so easy. You have to make split-second decisions: ticks, or a foot contorted between the boulders because you missed your stepping-stone. It was like playing hop-scotch all day.

Fortunately these ticks (the *Ixodidae*) only feed three times during their lives, first as larvae which feed in order to moult, then as nymphs which can only become adult after a gorge of blood, and finally as adults when the fertilised female needs blood before she can produce eggs. The ticks usually drop off the host between feeds so that three different host animals are involved. Most of the tick's life is thus spent in waiting for a host to pass within grabbing distance. If necessary they can wait years without any food or drink. Equally remarkable is the fact that during this time they don't become dried out, for they often live in very hot, arid grasslands. It is one of those laws of mathematics that small objects have a larger surface area relative to their volume than bigger ones of a similar shape. Tiny animals therefore have an enormous surface, relatively speaking, through which to dry out and small desert animals can usually only survive by spending the heat of the day below ground or beneath stones. Ticks spend much of their time sitting at the top of grass blades in the sun. Obviously their wax-coated cuticle is extremely efficient in preventing water loss but when they do become dehydrated they crawl down to ground level and are able actively to absorb moisture through their skins from humid air!

We acted as hosts for thousands of larvae and hundreds of nymphs and adults. The adults were rather more than one-eighth of an inch long, shiny brown and pear shaped. They would hang on for days if you let them, steadily gorging blood. The poor old mules became horribly infested and there was nothing we could do about it. It was difficult enough de-ticking ourselves, even with repellent on to start with. When they feed, ticks make a minute incision and insert their proboscis without one's feeling it. A gummy saliva sets hard and holds the tick in place; there are barbs too, for good measure. Pulling the ticks off leaves the mouthparts stuck in the skin and the irritation persists. We scratched for weeks after visits to Nachisar.

It was clearly better to have hooves on the lava flows, for the zebras (of which there were about 400 on the plains) galloped over the stuff with no difficulty at all. More impressive still were the greater kudu. They are not uncommon in Ethiopia and at Nachisar scores of them lived in the thorn thicket, a fearful lacerating tangle of thorns and spines which clothes the steep scarp between the plains and the lakeside. Only once did I leave the path on the escarpment and it took me five painful hours to find a way out again. One of the dominant bushes is *Acacia mellifera*, a type which I think qualifies very well for the name 'wait-a-bit' thorn. The pairs of hooked thorns clutch at skin and clothing so that every movement to extricate oneself generally makes the predicament worse. It is all too easy to end up in a ludicrous posture with no limbs free to move at all. From the ground the rigid, needle-tipped spikes of *Sanseveria* plants rise up to spear one's legs. In this seemingly impenetrable thicket the greater kudu can disappear with astonishing facility. Even the huge bulls with their great spiral horns can vanish without leaving a detectable path in their wake. They can even do it quietly. To find them where we could look at them we used to sit and watch the edge of the thicket in the early mornings and evenings. They would emerge with slow unhurried movements to stand and browse in the open during the most pleasant times of the day.

Very few antelopes are quite as stately as a bull greater kudu. The horns, measured around the spirals, can reach five feet or more in length. There are neat, white chevrons on the face and the powerful neck is hung beneath with a shaggy fringe running down to the dewlap and enhancing the impression of depth and strength. The colour overall is greyish-brown with vertical white flank stripes; this varies with the locality for kudu range from the Sudan to South Africa.

The shores of the lakes were rocky for the most part but there were bays with dark-coloured sand and low, waterside trees. Round much of the periphery a narrow border of rushes grew as an evergreen band and in shallow places reeds and rushes filled the bays to form a swamp where the hippos ploughed channels and opened up places to fish. We used to favour *Tilapia* for a good camp-fire supper but we tried everything that could be landed on the same light tackle, and once, in my finest hour, that included a thirty-pounder. The late evenings in camp could make up for a whole day of parching discomfort. I would sit on a rock at the water's edge fishing gently and easily, not really seeking great excitement. A smooth cast, the plop of the bait, unseen things fidgeting in the reeds, hippos grunting somewhere along the shore, the smell of wood-smoke and, on the best days, there would be a satisfying sunset and an arching, springing rod in my hand.

Fishing means very different things to different people. The crew of one boat I saw sought only a record Nile perch. They anchored in the bays, hurling lines and hooks about which looked as though they had come off a crane, and buoying up the live bait with oil-can floats. Not content with half a dozen gaffs, they carried revolvers too.

In contrast to the brown water of Abaya, Chamo is a clear lake, and on hot still days it was almost irresistibly inviting. But we never gave in to the temptation. The risk of bilharzia, a debilitating disease, the cure of which is reputed to be worse than the symptoms, was just too discouraging. The disease organism spends part of its life-cycle in a water snail and enters human tissue through the skin. There is no prophylactic and we had to boil or chlorinate all the water we used. Besides, there were crocodiles and even big ones have the most amazing powers of concealment. So we contented ourselves, at the end of those lakeside days, with sponging down and drying off in the breeze which usually came after sunset.

Despite the discomforts of being strictly terrestrial I was to spend many hours tramping around Nachisar and grew to be very fond of these plains. One interest in particular drew me to them whenever I could find an opportunity: Swayne's hartebeest. The word hartebeest comes from the Boers who thought the animals resembled stags. They have a wide range in Africa, occurring from Senegal, east to Ethiopia and south to the Cape. Swayne's used to be abundant in Somalia but they died in thousands during the rinderpest outbreaks of the 1890s and were finished off around the turn of the century by hunters using newly imported firearms. The total population of Swayne's hartebeest is now believed to consist of a few scattered herds in Ethiopia numbering perhaps 600 in all. The sub-species has consequently been listed as critically endangered in the IUCN Red Data Book.*

Swayne's is a distinctive type; the mature animals stand about fifty-one inches at the shoulder and are generally a chestnut colour with fawn hindquarters and a black stripe from shoulder to knee. There are often black markings on the hindlegs too, just above the hock, and sometimes a black smudge on the flanks. Bulls tend to be darker. There were, I think, almost a hundred of them at Nachisar, though it took some time to determine this. Herds would often be lying down in some hollow of the plains with only their heads visible above the grass. Once picked out through the glasses however their heads are quite unmistakable. The horns in both sexes grow from a high pedicle on the skull so that they diverge from a point well above the ears. The senses are so keen that when you first catch sight of the animals they are usually looking at you with their ears pricked, presenting two distinct pairs of appendages, one above the other.

The first animal in the herd to sense danger gives a loud nasal snort. At this signal the herd scrambles to its feet to assess

* IUCN Red Data Book, vol. 1, *Mammalia*, by Noel Simon, published by the International Union for Conservation of Nature and Natural Resources, Morges, Switzerland, 1966.

the threat, several or all of the adults taking up the alarm snort in turn. If the danger should already be too close for comfort, that is within the critical distance at which they normally take flight, the herd will gallop off, stopping to watch for a few minutes from a safer position, then continuing in more orderly fashion – often in single file behind an old female. With their high shoulders and sloping hindquarters they may look ungainly but they are certainly not slow. The problem in counting them on foot is to be able to recognise a group when it is next encountered two or three days later at the other end of the plains.

By creeping up-wind on hands and knees it is not difficult to get close to a resting herd of hartebeest, but not wishing to shoot them, which would be pathetically easy, I can't say I have often found it a very profitable exercise. In open grassland, crouching with your nose to the earth, you can't really see very much without being seen. Suddenly leaping up with a camera ought to be a good way of getting photographs at close range but I usually find I've misjudged the distance and nothing is in focus or else the sun is shining straight into the lens. More than once I have risen triumphant from the grass expecting to get the closest pictures ever, only to find either nothing at all or else the herd watching me with quiet curiosity from the top of the next rise.

One day, perhaps, people will photograph the hartebeest from cars but if so there will be no cattle on the plains and the wildlife will be assured of a future. At present, in addition to the pressure from domestic stock there is an ever-present threat from poachers. 'I was only trying to shoot a little one,' a local policeman explained when we caught him firing into a herd. The police, like the military, regard free game meat as one of the few perks attached to postings away from the towns.

At Nachisar about half a dozen men had been stationed in a huddle of shacks on a hill overlooking God's Bridge. It was a good vantage point but the police hadn't seen us arrive and I presented my authorising letter from the Provincial Governor only on the way back to Arba Minch. It was an eminently satisfactory situation for our safari was by then a *fait accompli*.

We had done all we wanted to do, our rations were finished and we were on our way home, but the police couldn't complain without admitting to maintaining an embarrassingly inefficient vigilance. So we sat for a little while and talked affably in our respective languages while Berhanu tried to act as interpreter, and a child (for there were wives and families there) stood, and stared, and sniffed; pouting his upper lip trying to control the streaming of his nose.

We never had occasion to pass the police post again for on subsequent visits to Nachisar it proved possible to operate from a series of lakeside camp sites which we reached by crossing the fifteen miles of lake in the aluminium boat brought from Abiata.

We had spent nearly a fortnight on our mule trek and the bridges, by the time we got back to them, were again in need of repair. The bundles of rushes had dried and shrivelled and would have to be replaced if the mules were not to put their hooves through the framework of branches below. We were all tired but we made the effort and when the restoration work was finished I decided that this time the mules could certainly carry their packs, at least across the first bridge which was only a few yards long and was built on to firm, level ground at either end. It seemed fairly safe but it was a wrong decision.

The big white mule needed no coaxing and I was confidently bringing the other one across when one of the logs rolled slightly beneath the layer of rushes. The mule went down hard. He was pitched on to his side with two legs through the bridge and an ever-widening gap beneath him as his thrashing body forced the logs further apart. Dodging the kicks, I fumbled with the buckles which held the canvas panniers to the pack saddle. Berhanu tried to quieten the animal. Jean was holding the big mule which was now safely between the two bridges. I had one pannier off, the other being completely inaccessible, when the bridge finally disintegrated and plunged the whole struggling heap of us into about ten feet of water.

Spluttering and gurgling, Berhanu tried to tether the mule to the remains of the bridge. I was still clinging to the pannier full of camping gear which I had unfastened. I hung on to the mule with my other hand. Luckily the current was slow but the river at this point had cut such a deep channel between vertical banks that I found it impossible to lift the sodden pannier up on to dry land; in fact I couldn't even raise it above water without submerging myself. Jean, lying on the bank and straining to reach down, eventually managed to catch one of the straps and dragged the soggy load up the bank. By now Berhanu had the other pannier off the mule and was calling for assistance. He didn't get any, for at this point Jean gave one horrified yell and disappeared from view.

The big mule had wandered off and Jean had seen him standing in the middle of the second bridge fully loaded and undecided whether to attempt to climb the sloping tree trunk which led off the bridge at the far side, or whether to try to turn round and come back. To try to turn round would be disastrous. He had to go forward and needed to be led. By the time I had scrambled out of the water and taken in the situation, Jean was already trying to get to his head. It was too late: he was turning. A tremendous splash and Jean was in the river with the mule on top of her. To make matters worse they had gone in downstream of the bridge so that the current, which in the main branch of the river was fast and powerful, was carrying them away from the bridge. On the other side it would have held them against it.

Jean surfaced and with a few strokes swam back to the bridge. Apart from a badly bruised leg she was unhurt. The mule, trying unsuccessfully to gain a foothold at the river bank, was allowing himself to be carried downstream by the current. There was a swirling in the water behind him; crocodiles were following. After about sixty yards he was swept around a bend in the river and lost from our view.

The riverside vegetation was almost as difficult and painful to penetrate as thorn thickets had been. It took nearly two hours of wriggling, crawling and hacking before the mule was located. It had been killed and disembowelled. Caught up in some tree roots it was lying within a few yards of a gently-shelving stretch where it might easily have walked ashore. Surprisingly, not much equipment had been lost although some of the leather pack straps had been bitten through as cleanly as if they had been cut with a knife.

Between the two bridges, or rather bridge and a half, the smaller mule shook himself like a dog and calmly started to graze. Berhanu had organised a gang of passers-by into hauling the animal out of the water by its harness. It didn't seem in the least upset by it all and at once allowed itself to be led across the catwalk and on to Arba Minch. We left Jean, still a little tearful, surrounded by saturated bedding, clothing and tentage which she had spread in the afternoon sun to dry. With supreme optimism she was also trying to salvage some of the dripping plant specimens which had been so carefully dried in the press. It was an unhappy incident but I felt relief, more than anything, at the fact that Jean had proved to be a strong swimmer.

Labouring up the hill to Arba Minch I considered how I should break the news to the owner. Like most Ethiopian policemen, he spoke no English. Berhanu would have to interpret. As it happened we didn't have to say much; the *farenge* had come back covered in cuts and scratches, with his shirt all torn and with only one mule. The details didn't matter.

'*Nega*,' said the policeman. Tomorrow. 'Then we will talk, today it is too late.'

His expression was serious but he was unable to conceal a flicker of satisfaction. Litigation is virtually an Ethiopian sport and haggling over compensation was a treat to be made the most of. Berhanu slowly shook his head.

'It will be the high price,' he murmured.

I fetched the Land-Rover which had been parked outside the Governor's office and we drove back to the Collofu River to collect Jean and our belongings.

'I've been thinking,' she said as she limped about helping to pack up the things, 'and I've decided it's time you got a good job in insurance or something.'

I was relieved to see a rueful smile. An hour and a half later we checked into the hotel.

At the hotel in Arba Minch you can always be sure of fresh fish; nearly thirty species have been recorded in the lakes. There had been a fishing party on the lakes that weekend and suspended from a rope outside the hotel was a fish-head about the size of a bucket. The perch must have weighed considerably more than the man who caught it. Later, in the bar, I got into conversation with the anglers on the subject of fish, fishing and crocodiles. Jean, who had had enough of crocodiles for a bit, chatted to the hotel manageress.

'It's obvious', said one of the fishermen with a scarlet bald head and a German accent, 'that those crocodiles must be eating tons of fish; they should be thinned out.'

Having only just got my top lip stuck in a long-awaited mug of beer I didn't really feel like arguing, but there was no evidence that I could think of to support his point of view. In the first place they had been thinned out; skin-hunters had only a few years before given up full-time operations on the lakes. As I was to discover later, the density of crocodiles in the Collofu River was much higher than existed anywhere else around the shores.

Like most problems in ecology, it was a complex one. Crocodiles at different stages of their life history will eat anything from insects and spiders to very large mammals. They catch live prey, they eat carrion and they eat each other. Many of the animals which they eat are themselves predatory upon other creatures or their eggs, or are cannibals.

What good is a crocodile anyway? It's a reasonable question to ask but it is the sort of question which often seems to arise from an underlying notion that wild animals somehow ought to be useful to man in order to justify their existence. It is not sufficient that they, like us, evolved to fill a particular role in nature, a niche. From a purely ecological point of view it is just as reasonable to ask what good is man to a crocodile.

The fact is that crocodiles and their prey all interact with one another in an extremely complicated web of food relationships and it is very difficult to assess what effect, if any, a certain species has upon the numbers of another. Baby crocodiles eat so many water creatures which feed on fish eggs and fry, that we can't even be sure whether, on balance, a crocodile is harmful or beneficial in a fishery; ecologically that is, they certainly don't do the fishing nets any good. They obviously serve a function as scavengers and might benefit fisheries by helping to keep a desirable balance between the different species of fish. In some waters where crocodiles have been studied it has been found that they eat mainly the low value fish such as catfish which are known to take a heavy toll of the more valuable types.

Crocodile-skin goods bring fancy prices in western markets but only the belly-skin is used, the rest of the animal is wasted. The biggest belly-skins naturally bring the highest prices but from what is already known of crocodile ecology the skin-hunters look like having to face some very hard facts if they hope to stay in business. Crocodiles mature slowly; they take as long to reach sexual maturity as do human beings and can take much longer. There is a definite breeding season. The mother crocodile buries her eggs in the earth and guards the nest from marauding storks, baboons, hyaenas and, in particular, monitor lizards. The eggs take three months to hatch. At the end of the incubation period the youngsters can be heard croaking and the mother digs up the eggs and leads or even carries the foot-long hatchlings to water. They have been seen to stay together with her for several weeks after that. If a nesting mother should be shot, her clutch is almost certainly doomed.

Apart from man, adult crocodiles have very few enemies and most natural mortality occurs among the very young ones. Furthermore the older and bigger the crocodile, up to a point, the more eggs she lays in a clutch. It is not surprising therefore that the intensive hunting of crocodiles with a premium on the larger ones has already wiped out the Nile crocodile from many parts of its range and stocks are rapidly declining elsewhere.

Probably the only long-term future for the Nile crocodile and the skin industry lies in artificially increasing crocodile numbers in suitable localities. The species has bred in captivity but more easily the eggs of wild ones can be collected and hatched in enclosures. The young may then be cared for during their vulnerable infant stage. When they are past this initial danger period they can be released to look after themselves. A year of protection would probably enormously improve the chances of survival and the extra crocodiles resulting from this 'farming' could be calculated, and an annual yield of skins worked out on a safe, sustained basis. Commercially, different systems have already been tried and in parts of southern Africa it pays to rear young crocodiles for three years before releasing them to maintain the wild population. Those destined for market are kept until they reach cropping size at about five years old.

We had arranged to meet the policeman at 9 a.m., he was on time and off duty. We exchanged brief formalities and waited for him to name his price. He said nothing; he and Berhanu stood gazing absently at the passers-by.

'Well, how much is it to be?' I asked impatiently.

Would we like some coffee? No, thanks, we had just had some.

Mules were very hard to get in Arba Minch.

Yes, I knew that: 'How much?'

It had been a very good mu . . .

'How much?'

He stared at the ground and with the deliberation of a poker-player said, '*Amist meto burr.*' Five hundred dollars. It was obviously going to take even longer than I'd expected. Berhanu's discreet enquiries had turned up a current market price of about a hundred and twenty. A couple of hours later we were down to three hundred.

'All right,' I said, 'tell him we'll go to court.'

'Two fifty,' came the reply, and that was his last price. Court it was. I recalled the familiar sight of milling crowds around a courthouse. It was the last thing I really wanted.

To my great relief I found that for settling minor disputes there was a special 'Court of the People' which would spare me a protracted ordeal in the court proper. It had no authority and gave no binding rule. It was merely an arrangement for obtaining independent judgements which the disputants were expected to accept; a sort of arbitration.

Uptown and downtown Arba Minch are completely separate. They are also up and down in the physical sense as well as in American parlance. Proceedings were conducted by a police officer in a subsidiary police station, a '*chika*' hut with a tin roof at the bottom of the hill. A youth and a man were brought in from among the idlers outside, and they were joined by two policemen. This constituted the 'court'. Each member was then called upon to give his name and to state how long he had lived in Arba Minch. There then followed a brief whispered conference in the corner of the room and the judgement was announced. One hundred and sixty dollars. No complaints. The whole procedure took less than half an hour.

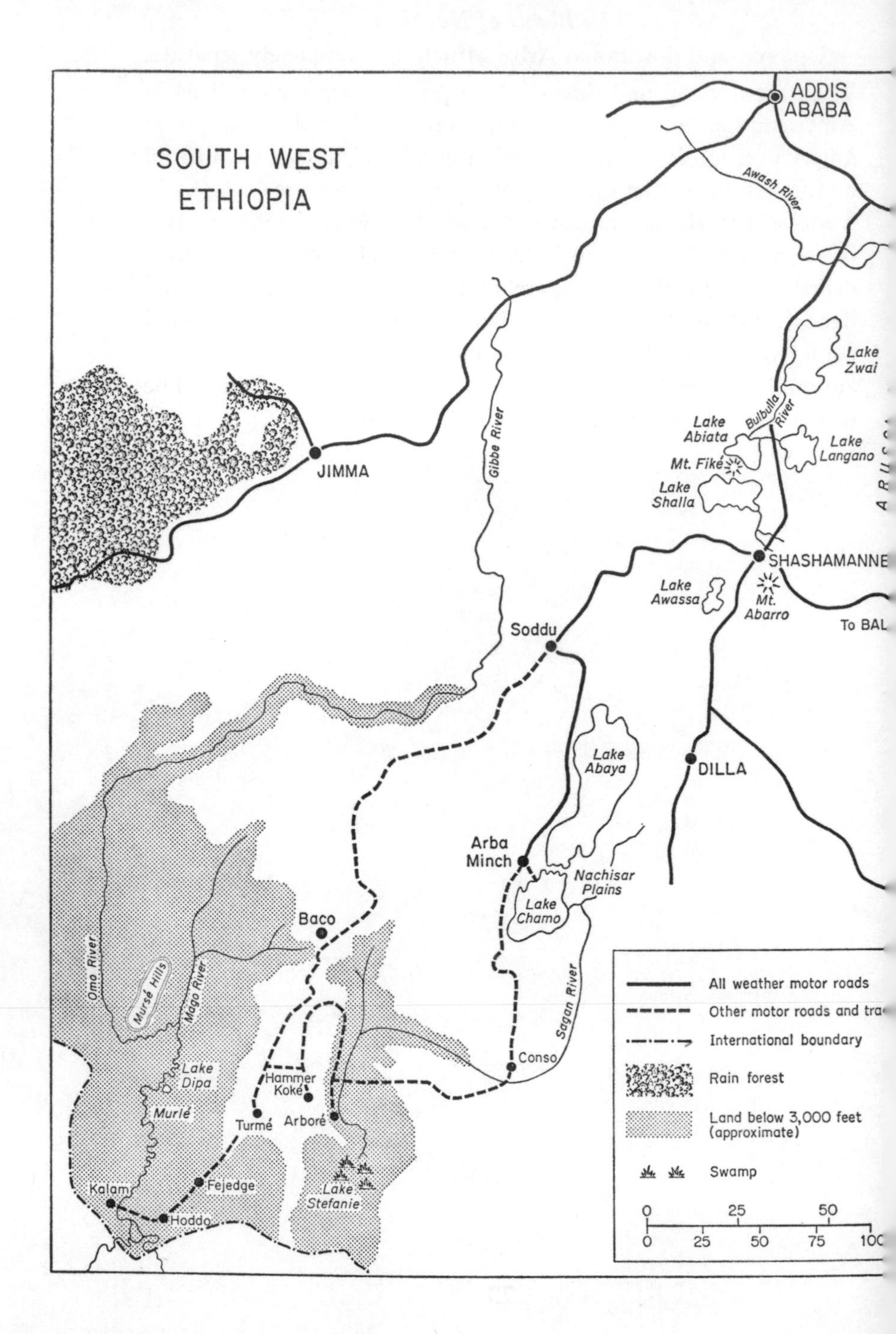

SOUTH WEST
ETHIOPIA
ADDIS
ABABA
Awash River
JIMMA
Gibbe River
Lake
Zwai
Bulbulla
River
Lake
Abiata
Lake
Langano
Mt. Fiké
Lake
Shalla
SHASHAMANNE
Lake
Awassa
Mt.
Abarro
To BAL
Soddu
Lake
Abaya
DILLA
Arba
Minch
Nachisar
Plains
Lake
Chamo
Baco
Omo River
Mursé Hills
Mago River
Sagan River
Lake
Dipa
Hammer
Koké
Conso
Murlé
Turmé
Arboré
Kalam
Fejedge
Hoddo
Lake
Stefanie
All weather motor roads
Other motor roads and tra
International boundary
Rain forest
Land below 3,000 feet
(approximate)
Swamp
0 25 50
0 25 50 75 100

4

The South-West

It was June. In Addis Ababa the water was running in torrents through the streets and the people bore an air of dejection. Three more months of it. The big rains normally last until *Maskal* in late September, a time of great religious significance and festivity which follows close upon the Ethiopian New Year, but a long time off for the thousands who were squelching barefoot in the mud.

On any given day of the year, somewhere in Ethiopia it is likely to be raining while in another part the sun can be blazing through moistureless air and the rocks can be too hot to touch. In a vast, dissected land which ranges from below sea-level to 15,000 feet above, a varied rainfall pattern is to be expected and has to be taken into account whenever a long journey is planned. But it is not always possible to avoid the rain entirely. On all-weather roads of course it makes no difference but then made-up roads are few and far between. In the far south-west, reputed to be one of the richest big-game areas in the country, it would be dry and a good time to work, but getting there would mean negotiating some very wet highlands.

In difficult terrain two vehicles are much better than one, and as it happened, an enterprising Scot by the name of Roger Mackay was arranging a hunting safari in the south-west at the same time that I was planning our fieldwork. My assignment was to carry out an ecological recce of the east side of the lower Omo River from Lake Rudolf northwards into the valley of the River Mago and eastwards to the Lake Stefanie Rift. We agreed to travel together and left Addis by the main road south on 17 June. The hunters' camp had already left by truck several days before, and Roger, accompanied by his client (a medical man from Montana inevitably known as 'Doc') and four Ethiopian assistants, drove only a small jeep. Jean, Tadessa (a chubby little Amhara chap who was our assistant for the trip) and myself crowded into the Land-Rover together with enough camping equipment for a two-month safari. A fast uneventful drive brought us by evening to Soddu and in the hotel that night we drank a toast to the journey and talked for an hour before turning in. Doc was an interesting character; a short man, bald, softly spoken but with a lively sense of humour. He had come for a two-week safari. He had hunted before in East and central Africa so he was no novice but south-west Ethiopia was virtually unknown country and the adventure of hunting in a wild and remote region had an appeal of its own. As a professional hunter, Roger's job was to accompany Doc, and in due course other clients, as they went out hunting. He was expected to advise on where and what to shoot. Roger was employed by a safari outfitter who had laid on the transport, tentage, food and other necessary equipment for the safari. At the moment a whole truckload of it was somewhere on the road ahead. The outfitter had already done a reconnaissance east of the Omo River – enough to be able to say that it was worth operating a hunting business there. Doc had duly paid his fees and made his way to Ethiopia as the first client. None of us in the hotel that night had ever been in south-west Ethiopia before.

The following morning we left the hotel and the south road and took a small track marked by a blank sign on a stick. It might have said Baco at one time for there is a sizeable village of that name (though it is called Jinca by everyone who lives there) about 150 miles further on.

At Baco there is an important police post which receives a monthly supply of provisions by truck from Addis. The track was well-defined to say the very least. The wheels of the big Fiat and Mercedes trucks had worn ruts so deep into the track that the axles had begun to gouge out a third channel between the ruts. There were long stretches of fine black clay – black cotton soil, as it is often called from its resemblance to the soil of the cotton-growing districts of India. When wet it has the consistency and slipperiness of butter. Straddling the ruts we slithered and skidded along quite successfully for encouragingly long spells at a time until one or other of the vehicles came to a halt by sliding sideways into a rut and coming to rest at forty-five degrees. On the downhills it was sometimes possible to continue sliding in this position and eventually get upright again. When necessary, we linked up by cable and the one pulled the other out. Mostly I was the one who needed pulling out for Roger's cargo was readily convertible into pushing-power whereas ours was mostly dead-weight. The first real obstacle was the first ford, and that only held us up for half a day. The river was nearly three feet deep in parts and running fast. 'Maximum advisable fording depth is one and a half feet,' I once read in a handbook. 'Avoid overspeeding . . . Drive slowly and surely.'

'I reckon we ought to rush it,' shouted Roger, already reversing his jeep for the charge. I took a light reading and focused the camera on where I estimated the engine would drown. *Rrrrmmmm Rrrrmmmm . . . Whooooosh.* Hurtling forward from a racing start the jeep hit the water and completely disappeared under a bow-wave. By the time it reappeared it was sitting high and dry at the foot of the incline on the far side, all four wheels spinning ineffectually and the chassis resting solidly on a ridge between two ruts.

There was a lot of pushing and revving and clouds of blue smoke, but in the end the jeep had to be winched and it was some considerable time later that it topped the slippery incline and it was my turn to ford the river.

Having taken every standard precaution plus a few of my own to keep water out of the vital parts I engaged low-ratio second gear and drove steadily into the river. No trouble. Apart from a slight list to starboard she was going beautifully. A little care and thought always pays dividends. Skill, not rashness, gets one across rivers. I could see where I was going and with everything under control I came cautiously and firmly to a complete stop in exactly the same position as Roger's flying jeep had done several hours before.

'Not much in it really,' Roger remarked, 'you might as well rush it, it's quicker.'

There were more rivers and innumerable streams to be crossed but somehow we managed to keep going. The track wound on past little groups of huts with patches of cultivation; through hamlets where *chika* houses lined the track and people stared while dogs and children called and ran behind; through damp valleys and over hills clothed with a green savanna of *Combretum* and *Terminalia* trees. Oribi and bohor reedbuck bounded away, their brown heads bobbing above the long grass. We crossed the Dami and Mazi Rivers, beautiful forested tributaries of the Omo River. We drove along their shingle beds to find the way out through the tall clumps of reed mace and *Saccharum* grass whose silky, silvery inflorescences nodded like ostrich plumes in the cool shade beneath the riverside trees. I resolved to return one day to the Mazi River and stay there for a time – and I did. Waterbuck and buffalo lived by the water and tsetse flies kept the cattle away. At night lions roared and we heard the hoarse coughing of a leopard, encouraging sounds when one is looking for game. On the grassland close by there were herds of hartebeest and a family of cheetah.

We saw none of this on our first drive through but that evening, before pitching camp, we met our first traffic. A truck came grinding along towards us. It stopped and a wiry Italian leant out from the shaking cab and shouted a greeting above the noise of the clapped-out diesel.

'*Saluté*,' 'Hello,' '*Tenastilin*.'

It became apparent that Amharic was the only language we had in common so we left the conversation to Tadessa who was the only one able to translate it into English.

'Ask him what the road's like ahead.'

There was a long stream of Amharic to which the Italian nonchalantly waved his hand in reply.

'*Minim yellum*' he yelled. Nothing to it; that much I understood.

'*Buzu chika?*' I ventured – much mud?

'*Tinnish bicha*' – only a little.

Good. Things were looking up. Perhaps we had passed the worst. We parted with warm '*Ciaos*' and the lorry pulled away with a din like a road drill. One of Roger's crew was a good cook and that evening Jean sat in unaccustomed luxury and had nothing to do with the stove.

There was no rain during the night and we continued next morning in a mood of optimism which prevailed undiminished for the best part of an hour. It began to fade when Roger succeeded once more in positioning his jeep upon a ridge with all its wheels off the ground. It was an open stretch where the truck-drivers during the wettest periods had made detours to avoid the ruts. The result was a multiplication of ruts with the ridges between not even parallel. Roger had found himself driving along a gradually narrowing ridge which eventually fitted snugly between his wheels and left the jeep mounted like a hover-train. I managed to perform a very similar trick about half a mile further on and thereafter it was one delay after another as the obstacles got progressively worse. There were times when Jean couldn't bear to look. Doc came over once while they were digging and pushing at Roger's jeep. He took Jean's wrist and felt her pulse, looking grave.

'Either my watch has stopped or your wife has passed away,' he said.

At one point the track disappeared into a water-filled crater and the only way around it was over a ditch. Roger, predictably, decided to rush it. His idea this time was that if he got up enough momentum he could jump the gap. He nearly did it too, but not quite. The jeep dived into the side of the ditch, came almost to the vertical then slid down nose-first. It was very spectacular to watch. Roger crawled out, reeling not so much from the impact, for which he had braced himself, but from an ammunition box which had caught him unaware in the back of the neck. He couldn't help looking comic. His thick glasses had slid down his nose but were held on by a string round the back of his head. He slapped on his floppy bush hat and adjusted the 'Safari Africa' sign to the front. He was, I imagine, about forty, bearded and with an irrepressibly ebullient character.

'Let's get winching!' he shouted.

It was less than ten miles to Baco, when on a steep pass there was a terribly final sort of noise from the rear axle and the Land-Rover came abruptly to a halt. One of the differential gears had fractured. We still had front-wheel drive but it was hopelessly inadequate under the circumstances.

Luckily, Roger was in front at the time and from the switch-back track he could look down from a point directly above.

'What's wrong?' he bawled.

'We've only got front-wheel drive.'

Five minutes later the jeep came bouncing backwards down the narrow pass and for his final stunt Roger towed the Land-Rover over thirteen kilometres of indescribable road into Baco. It was dark by the time we got there and the 'hotel' was a disappointment. It had run out of beer and by the light of the paraffin lamps the rooms, which were like cubicles in a *chika* lean-to outside, looked horridly verminous. We continued through the village and camped by the airstrip. It rained all night.

'What do you plan to do?' Doc enquired next morning as the hunting party prepared to leave. I said that as soon as I'd discovered what spares were needed I would radio Addis and try to get them flown in. Doc glanced at the wall of mountains to the north and stared at the portable transceiver. He looked dubious as he shook hands.

'I guess you'll be here a while,' he said in his quiet drawl. He scuffed the rich damp earth with his foot. 'But your crops should do well,' he added.

The damage to the Land-Rover was worse than I had expected. The pieces of broken gear had ground around the works until there was hardly a gear-wheel left undamaged. It would have to be a complete new rear axle assembly. We strung the radio aerial as high in a tree as we could and at 9 a.m., the pre-arranged contact time, I switched on hopefully and bellowed into the set. A tiny crackling voice came back in reply. 'You're very faint,' it said, 'you'll have to speak up.' We were in direct contact with John Blower at Wildlife HQ in Addis. The ensuing conversation left me in a state of near-collapse but the message got through. John was now aware that we were stranded in Baco and needed a new axle. If there was one to be had in Addis, I knew I could depend on John to get it to us.

By daylight Baco proved to be a bigger place than it had seemed the night before. The police station was, by our standards, an army barracks inside a wired compound complete with sentry box and armed guards. We went there after meeting the Baco Governor, a helpful man. At his suggestion the police officer in charge of transport agreed to help with the car repairs when the spares arrived. In the afternoon Jean and I sauntered about the town with nothing in particular to do. There was a large village square surrounded by bars and small traders' stores mostly kept by Arabs, it appeared. They were the usual *chika* buildings with tin roofs and earth floors which sold non-perishable sundries ranging from sandals and *shammas* to spices and paraffin lamps. Jean was keen to buy fresh fruit but there wasn't any. Fresh food was always a problem. There was a butcher's shop though and since the locals made no distinction between one piece of meat and another Jean managed to extract a whole fillet steak from a half cow for what others paid for the same weight of scrag. We ate well that night for we still had vegetables which we'd brought from Addis. Tomorrow, they said, we could buy vegetables in Baco for it was market day.

All the following morning little streams of people trickled into Baco from the adjacent hills and the square gradually became a jostling, crowded market-place. From all directions they came, women bent double under baskets and bundles, empty-handed men striding along for the drinking and the company, people riding or driving donkeys and mules, dogs and children tagging along for whatever they might find. The women settled down, cross-legged beneath the trees of the market square, and spread their pathetic little piles of produce on rugs and skins. Tiny stacks of onions sorted at so many cents a pile, garlic cloves, stunted potatoes and bendy carrots, corn cobs, grain and mysterious bits of shrivelled roots and leaves for seasoning. Some, whose subsistence livelihood left no surplus at all, offered only bundles of firewood. Even allowing for the tinkers who had kettles, tin mugs, door hinges and rusty nails, one got the impression that a few pounds would have bought the entire market.

As the *tej** and *talla*** drinkers began reeling from the bars we strolled back to camp, glad that it was twenty minutes away and invisible until you were nearly there. We had a very quiet night.

The repair business went more smoothly and quickly than we ever hoped for or thought possible. The axle arrived by DC-3 after two days and the chief mechanic took over the job of fitting it for us.

The mechanic was a jolly, chuckling character, black as coal with no front teeth. He had lived in Baco for many years maintaining the supply trucks and was a fund of local stories and information. He had the Land-Rover ready for the road on the fourth day, and over a sundowner in the local bar we asked him about the journey ahead.

We should keep going south as far as a place called Turmé. At Turmé there was a police post and the police would direct us to the track which ran west to the Omo River. There were plenty of wild animals near the Omo, he assured us, and some very wild people. Tadessa translated this last piece of information with evident concern but he made no comment.

We left Baco next morning with mixed feelings but with a general underlying apprehension. On the 1:500,000 War Office map (still the best maps there are for most of Ethiopia) there was no village of Turmé and no road south out of Baco. This fact alone didn't worry us; it probably just meant that in 1938 when the Italians did the original mapping, the village and the track didn't exist. The disturbing thing was that south of Baco a large area had been left white and the words 'very mountainous' and 'impracticable' printed across it.

Jean, who had been rather quiet throughout the trip, said simply that if there was a road (and if there wasn't, what had happened to the hunting party?) it couldn't possibly be any

* *Tej*—an Ethiopian version of mead.
** *Talla*—a crude beer, usually brewed from barley.

worse than the one we'd just come along from Soddu. Tadessa, since his chat with the mechanic, had things other than road conditions to worry about. I noticed that he had his ·38 revolver, which had previously been packed away in his luggage, now jammed close at hand in the door pocket. Admittedly, the natives of south-western Ethiopia have a reputation for savagery which rivals that of the Danakil, but when they go on the rampage they do so in large, heavily-armed bands and I couldn't see what good a revolver was going to do.

'It is only for the very last,' Tadessa said, rather self-consciously.

There was a track, and somehow it found a way through the mountains. It was rough and it was rocky. In Addis some months later we met a man who bore permanent scars from having once travelled it. His vehicle had rolled over. For us, however, having driven from Soddu at the height of the rains, the track was a relief: we had experienced worse. The broadleaf trees steadily gave way to acacias, and the last traces of cultivation dwindled away as the heavy, dark earth of the Baco highlands became browner and lighter and the track descended towards the dry southern lowlands.

We reached Turmé the following day, having clocked 133 kilometres, 83 miles, from Baco. There wasn't much there. A shack at the top of a slight incline flew the Ethiopian flag and must therefore be the police station. A twin row of dwellings leading up to it demarcated the main street. There was nothing else.

There were perhaps a dozen policemen at the outpost, twice as many as there are at some remote stations, but they had no form of transport and I don't recall that they had any radio communication. It was hard to see what their functions were. No doubt they maintained law and order among the Turmé residents, they represented an official 'presence' in the area and perhaps by just sitting and gossiping they collected useful intelligence about the activities of the local tribesmen.

When the formalities were over and our documents had been scrutinised, we asked about the track west. There was general agreement that we'd passed it, on our right a few kilometres back. Only three of the policemen had ever been along it. One was confident that the Omo could be reached by car in half a day. Another was equally certain that it was all of 200 kilometres and we'd be lucky to get there the next day. The third couldn't remember much about it. It was important because the last source of petrol had been at Soddu and if there really was another 200 kilometres to go we were destined to run out of fuel in the middle of nowhere. At the hunters' camp by the river we had two drums of fuel which had been sent by truck. The map suggested that if it was 200 kilometres it would have to be a very devious track and in arid lowlands tracks are usually fairly direct. We took heart at this and sped back down the main street to find our turning.

'Chickens!' Jean exclaimed as three or four scraggy bantams streaked across in front of the Land-Rover. 'This will be the last place to buy eggs.'

We bought up all the eggs in Turmé, some of which, judging by the trouble they had collecting them, hadn't quite been laid, and I think it came to nine. For the future we also asked if they ever had vegetables for sale. '*Yellem*.' 'Fruit?' '*Yellem*.' The word means no, nothing, negative: there had been times in Addis when I had believed it to be the standard Amharic reply to all queries.

The track wasn't difficult to find. We had only missed it before because we had been looking at a flock of vulturine guinea-fowl on the other side of the road. With their bald heads and long mantle of white-splashed, cobalt-blue feathers, they are curious, eye-catching birds.

The Omo River rises in the central highlands where they call it the Gibbe. It rushes south and west through deep gorges then bends finally southwards and, without leaving Ethiopia, meanders slowly and tortuously into the northern end of Lake Rudolf and hence into Kenya. Actually only the northern tip of Rudolf lies within Ethiopia. Almost all the 160 miles of its length are in Kenya's Northern Frontier province. Tourists are being flown there now, in regular flights from Nairobi, to fish in the lake and enjoy camping luxury in Kenya's remotest National Park.

One day it may be an International Park with organised launch trips up the lower Omo.

In 1965 Major Ian Grimwood and Leslie Brown visited the plains to the west of the lower reaches of the river. On a UNESCO wildlife advisory mission to Ethiopia they flew to Maji and travelled south from there by jeep. They were impressed by what they saw. Huge herds of eland, Burchell's zebra, tiang, Grant's gazelle, hartebeest and oryx, together with smaller numbers of buffalo, giraffe, waterbuck and lesser kudu. Nothing rare but an appreciable variety of game, so Brown and Grimwood recommended that part of the area should be developed as a game reserve and eventually upgraded to National Park status. They also recommended that the east bank of the lower Omo should be surveyed – by somebody.

The hunters' camp was, as far as we knew, about forty miles north of Lake Rudolf. From that base-camp we would work southwards to the lake, east to Lake Stefanie and also northwards into the country opposite the proposed park. I was particularly interested to get into this latter stretch. A small river called the Mago flows southwards for about twenty-five miles through an uninhabited and virtually unexplored valley before swelling the waters of the Omo. It had looked very exciting through the window of an aeroplane some weeks earlier. Limited funds were available for air survey and I had already flown over the valley by chartered light aircraft.

We certainly hadn't seen much big game so far. A few devoted pairs of Guenther's dikdik had been spotted beneath the acacia bushes, gingerly sorting the leaves from the thorns with their elongated snouts. One or two lesser kudu and an occasional gerenuk had risked bolting across the track in front of us but that was about all.

Between them these antelopes browse the thornbush very efficiently, cropping all levels up to more than six feet from the ground. This height is reached by the spindly gerenuk which rears vertically on its hind legs and hooks its forelegs over the branches for support. '*Giraffengazelle*' the Germans call it and very aptly. Gerenuk are reddish-brown antelopes three feet or more at the shoulder but with a disproportionately long neck and legs. The muzzle is neatly pointed and they can select food from the densest thorn bushes. Gerenuk occur only in the Horn of Africa and are quite at home in degraded grasslands where over-grazing by domestic stock has ruined the pasture and led to the encroachment of thornbush. As a result gerenuk may be actually increasing their range by profiting from man's degradation of the land.

It is partly the spatial distribution of feeding which enables very large numbers of different herbivores to thrive in the same area. From the root-grubbing warthog and grazing antelopes to the lofty, browsing giraffe (unhappily, hunted almost to extinction in Ethiopia) there is every combination of grazer/browser and browser/grazer in between, each selecting its own particular food species. Among the grazing animals there is further ecological separation in the type of grass, the part of the plant or stage of growth which is selected and eaten. None of this is all that surprising, for the whole complex of African herbage and herbivores has evolved together and the system has been working itself out for a long time. It would be much more surprising, and a little suspect, to discover a wholesome and sustaining vegetarian diet, and then to find that no animal had ever evolved to eat it. Rather like finding an income tax loop-hole that no one had ever thought of, or a vacant seat on a rush-hour train.

There is no doubt that a variety of antelopes can produce much more meat from a given area of land than can cattle which all compete for exactly the same fodder. On the hot, dry plains of Africa it isn't just a question of nutrition. Cows (like sheep and goats) have been introduced to Africa by man quite recently in terms of the evolutionary time-scale. They are affected by diseases which the indigenous beasts can resist. They have to be watered regularly whereas there are good meat-producing antelopes which don't care whether they ever see water or not.

It is not difficult to demonstrate that over wide areas of Africa a much higher yield of good meat could be obtained from wild animals than from domestic ones. The problem is how to take advantage of the fact. Herding cows and eating beef are well-established practices and game meat will need skilful marketing if game ranching is to appear an attractive proposition. Even so, marketing problems can be overcome as some pilot schemes have demonstrated and there is a trend in South Africa for ranchers to re-introduce game animals on to their cattle ranges as a profitable sideline.

None of this however is likely to affect the lives of the nomads for whom cows mean wealth, prestige and a source of milk. There are pastoralists in Ethiopia who wouldn't dream of killing their cows for meat; they only eat them when they die from natural causes.

The track ran due west and after an hour or so brought us on to a gentle decline overlooking the plains. In the distance a dark green ribbon of trees snaked across the bush; it was the Omo. Although the river was a long way off, it was obviously not going to be anything like two hundred kilometres from Turmé. It turned out to be only fifty-nine.

As the track lowered us out of sight of the river, the bush began to thin out and where there had been almost bare ground beneath a straggling cover of bushes there were now, increasingly, open expanses of tawny grassland with scattered tall acacia trees and termite mounds rising in reddish spires up to 20 feet high. This was Murlé; it even said so on our map.

I estimated the average visibility distance on either side of the track and began to jot down what we saw over a 20-kilometre stretch: Grant's gazelle, 100; beisa oryx, 23; tiang, 32; hartebeest, 14; gerenuk, 4; lesser kudu, 1; ostrich, 7. With repetitions and a few trials off the track where possible, one can gain some idea of animal densities. We saw most of the plains animals that there were to be seen on that first drive in. Later the list was augmented by warthogs, an occasional Grevy's zebra, a family of bat-eared foxes, a serval and a cheetah. Lions were heard but never seen.

We didn't get to the hunters' camp as quickly as we ought to have done. This was partly because we kept stopping every few minutes to stare at something through the glasses, but mainly because the two sets of tyre marks which we had been following went off in different directions and we followed the wrong ones. Neither set had been made by a jeep.

The ones we followed led us too far north and finally disappeared into a circle of grass huts. Before we got to within fifty yards of the dwellings we were surrounded by naked tribesmen and dozens more were streaming towards us. A few carried rifles but most were armed with spears.

Tadessa stared, aghast, at the hands, noses, lips and chins flattened against the side-windows and became practically incoherent. He tried to advise us all at once and in a tremulous voice that it was a very bad place, we should go away immediately, there was no truck here and we should have taken the other turning.

There didn't seem much point in staying but before we left I wanted to know where we were.

'Try to ask them the name of this place,' I said.

Tadessa slid back the window a fraction of an inch and allowed about six words to escape. A youth was ushered to the fore and, to Tadessa's amazement, replied in Amharic. Kerre was the name of the village, or it might have been the name of the tribe. We left without sorting it out.

When we finally did arrive at the hunters' camp, Roger greeted us with a look of utter astonishment.

'But your back axle was bust,' he protested, as if we couldn't possibly be there.

We exchanged news of the last few days while a place was being cleared for our tent. Doc was out hunting with the Swiss safari outfitter who had driven the truckload of petrol and camping gear. Roger had caught up with the truck shortly after leaving Baco and had actually driven into camp in front of it, which explained why we hadn't been able to distinguish his tyre marks. The tracks which we had followed to Kerre had been made by another truck which the crocodile hunters had brought down to collect a load of belly-skins. The skins were stored just beyond Kerre.

Overlooking the Mago Valley

Orthodox priest carrying a fly whisk

Danakil appreciates a cigarette (note knife)

Hairdressing at a Danakil camp

It was a good camp site. On the bank of the Omo, a clearing had been hacked out of the forest beneath a sheltering canopy of *Tamarindus* and fig trees. The river itself was high and running swiftly, yet the thick, brown water slipped by silently, gliding between high green walls to a lake called the Jade Sea.

There is a powerful magic between these green, living walls which affects those who wander alone. It is peaceful there, soothing, but at the same time violent and exciting. Greyish heaps of crocodiles bask in the morning sun, jaws gaping. Perhaps, momentarily, those same jaws, now a shiny yellow-green, will emerge from the water and the writhing body of a catfish is tossed between the teeth and audibly smashed with a few snatching bites. Olive baboons suddenly shatter the silence with barking and screaming, then the branches are still and there is silence again. Was it a leopard or merely a family row? There is no way of telling; nothing moves except the turbid water. At such times, to a lonely, awed observer, the lower Omo River seems prehistoric.

The natives navigate the Omo in dugout canoes, the most unstable craft I've ever seen. It wasn't long before we began to receive regular visitors from across the river. They were from the Bumé tribe and looked exactly like the natives at Kerre. They were very dark-skinned and showed some of the long-limbed proportions of the Nilotic negroes but not nearly to the same degree as the pure Nilotes of the southern Sudan or that part of Ethiopia adjacent to the White Nile. Most of them were stark naked and all carried spears and small wooden stools. They had a penchant for spitting by squirting gobbets through their teeth.

Tadessa became quite friendly with them, eventually. I found him one day trying to teach them to draw with a pencil and paper: he wasn't having much success. He told me later that they couldn't represent even the simplest objects. They were actually coming to hunt, for they had, as they put it, 'finished all the animals' in their own area.

The lower Omo Valley is an awful complex of Nilo-Hamitic tribes and subtribes, none of whom seemed to be on very good terms with their neighbours. The Bumé would not normally, I gathered, have dared to hunt at Murlé for this was too close to Hammer country. According to intelligence gathered by Tadessa, the Bumé were pretty confident that they would be safe if they stayed close to the *farenge* camp.

The Hammer are the most powerful, well-armed warriors in the south-west and Murlé was on the edge of Hammer country; not over-hunted by the Hammer but frequented by them often enough to keep the Bumé away. Almost a no-man's-land. Possibly this situation had helped to preserve the wildlife. Long may it last. There were laws against killing game without a licence but law enforcement in such places was impossible without a resident warden and a good team of guards. Even then it was difficult enough.

The Bumé hunting technique was effective and effortless. In the late afternoon they would stroll out on to the plains and set plaited rawhide snares along the game trails. The snares were attached to wooden stakes sunk into the ground. The following morning they would lie in the shade of a tree and watch the sky for circling vultures. When the vultures indicated that some wretched animal had been caught they ran out to spear it to death. They would return, spattered with blood and carrying hunks of meat. Giblets were carried wrapped in the animal's skin. Cooking was minimal. Pieces of meat were held over a fire for a few minutes and the warriors spent the rest of the day sleeping off the meal – that is until snare-setting time again.

Half a dozen poachers using this method caught more meat than they could possibly eat. Up to four antelopes a day; young, old, nursing mothers – the snares, of course, do not discriminate. One day we happened upon a tiang (a relative of the hartebeest) staggering over the plains with a wooden stake attached to its hind leg. We followed it in the Land-Rover until it finally flopped to the ground. It tried to stand at bay but was too tired even to stand. Luckily the rawhide thongs had not damaged the flesh and after we cut it free it made a complete recovery. If the Bumé had been able to obtain wire for making snares, its leg would have been severed.

The Bumé of course were innocently doing what primitive hunters have always done. Under primitive conditions they could continue doing it indefinitely but today, using rifles as well as ancient methods, they find that they finish all the animals. I doubt if they realise why; they cannot know that when hunting and gathering was the only human way of life the total world population was almost certainly less than the population of present-day Ethiopia – and that figure was added to the world's total in the last five months! Within Ethiopia there was little more than half the present population as recently as twenty-five years ago. It is easy to forget this and one often hears the remark 'but they've been doing it for thousands of years', meaning snaring, burning or whatever. It all comes down to numbers and even the tribes of the lower Omo are becoming too thick on the ground to live by wastefully hunting big game.

In fact, except where tsetse fly preclude it, pastoralism is now the normal way of life for most of these tribes – including the Hammer. Some of the small tribes along the Omo who do not keep cattle have recently begun to cultivate the terraces on and around the river bank. Their protein is derived mainly from fish which they catch with a sort of harpoon. At Kerre, since the crocodile hunters moved in, the staple diet of the natives has been crocodile meat.

During our attempts to get north into the Mago Valley we visited the crocodile hunters' camp, it being just about as far north as we managed to get. The camp followers from Kerre lay stretched about on the ground, heads resting on little carved stools, bellies bloated with crocodile meat. One or two of them rolled over or opened an eye to see what the disturbance was but most showed no sign of life.

Crocodile hunting is strictly night work and the hunters themselves, two Frenchmen, were also asleep when we arrived. They didn't seem to mind being roused; one of them had an outboard motor to repair before nightfall and said he was about to get up anyway.

The hunting is carried out from wooden flat-bottomed boats. The hunter stands in the prow with a spotlight powered by a car battery. As the crocodiles lie afloat in the water, their eyes reflect the beam of light. Behind the hunter, in the boat, the harpoonists crouch at the ready. With the crocodile's eyes held in the light it is possible to approach rapidly to within a few feet. At the last moment the hunter lifts his rifle and, at point-blank range, fires one soft-nosed bullet between the shining eyes. This is the cue for the harpoonist to make secure perhaps fourteen feet of flailing crocodile weighing as much as fifty stone before it has time to sink.

There is a tendency, after a water has been intensively hunted in this way, for the remaining crocodiles to be wary and to submerge before the hunter can get close enough. It would be interesting to know whether these shy survivors have learnt what is good for them or whether they were shy all the time and have consequently survived until the last. Not that it matters much. The hunting would have to continue through many generations of crocodiles in order to produce a wary breed. The record shows that they are likely to become locally extinct long before any selective pressures have time to show up.

The crocodile hunters showed me their catch for the last two and a half months. Stacked beneath a tarpaulin were five hundred belly-skins, salted and rolled like stair-carpets. The truck which had come to collect them was, like the outboard motor, in need of bush repairs. The driver was a small, wrinkled Italian called Giovanni.

The hunters had been operating on the Omo River for six years, gradually working upriver from Lake Rudolf. Most of their hunting was now being carried out far upriver from their present base-camp. I asked why they didn't move camp further north. The answer was that they couldn't get any further north with the truck. This was a blow. Giovanni had been forging tracks through the Ethiopian bush for thirty-three years. If he with a truckload of labourers couldn't get any further, we had no chance at all. The Mago would have to be reached on foot and without pack animals.

There was an excellent interpreter among the hunters' crew and I asked if the locals could be hired as porters. Not a hope.

The Mago Valley was in enemy territory. This left the river. We had no boat and the hunters had none to spare. With a fleet of dugout canoes we might be able to paddle up to the Mago River but we still wouldn't be able to move more than a day's walk from the river unless we carried supplies. In dense riverine forest a day's walk could mean a few hundred yards. The locals were not even happy about paddling so far up the river. The Mago Valley, it seemed, would have to remain unexplored.

When we got back to Murlé the hunters were chopping down trees and levelling the ground with shovels to make an airstrip. Another client was about to be flown in by chartered Cessna.

Personally I dislike shooting animals and although properly-controlled hunting does no harm to animal populations, I only shoot when I have to. At Murlé I shot an old bull hartebeest for the British Museum. It was a form of Swayne's-lelwel intergrade distinguished by the name of *neumani*. While I was skinning it, white-backed vultures were dropping out of the sky with a noise like six-inch shells. By the time I had finished, there must have been two hundred of them hunched on the acacias and standing around on the ground, silently watching.

Presumably each vulture, by flying to the area, gives the signal to the next one further off that carrion has been spotted. They could thus be drawn from miles away. Once on the carcass, hissing and squabbling over the entrails, they are very reluctant to leave and you can approach to within a few yards before they begin hopping and flapping away. You can drive them further back with each step towards them, but take a step or two backwards and they surge forward the same distance like an angry mob.

The meandering course of the lower Omo has produced many oxbows and backwaters, most of them now dry and overgrown, but just north of Murlé a small muddy lake is connected to the river by a narrow channel about two miles long. If the channel was dry it would be a useful path through the riverine forest and a convenient way to collect information on the fauna of the forest strip. When the work on the plains was finished I resolved to hack a way along the river bank until I came to the channel.

Jean decided to stay behind and bake bread in an ammunition box.

Expecting a long day, I set off one morning at dawn or at least early enough to see a pair of Pell's fishing owls returning, presumably from a night's hunting on the river. They spent the day close to our camp but I never had the luck to see them fishing. When I eventually reached the channel I found it mostly dry and followed it all the way to the lake. I got covered with red, biting ants which showered from the trees, an unidentified snake trickled across my boot and I was stung behind the ear by a hornet or something very similar.

For my trouble I found that the forest contained waterbuck bushbuck, buffalo, vervet monkeys, colobus monkeys and de Brazza's monkeys; all of which I knew were there anyway.

When I got back to camp I discovered that my little trip had caused some consternation. Tadessa, it was related, had tried to follow me. He had traced my footprints to where I had emerged on the river bank, but could trace them no further. Clearly, I had come to a tragic end. Before breaking the news he had sought a second opinion. Tadessa took a Bumé hunter to the spot and asked him to interpret the tracks. Just as he had suspected, the *farenge* had been dragged into the river. So it was that Jean was solemnly informed of my demise.

Not for nothing had Jean been made something or other in the Girl Guides. Back at the river bank it took her only two or three minutes to show where I had penetrated the impenetrable on hands and knees. To be truthful, Jean isn't really anything special at tracking at all; Tadessa and the Bumé must have been utterly useless.

That night I was able to settle a heated argument between two of the hunting fraternity. One of them insisted that the scrotum of a vervet monkey (which they called green monkey) was green, hence the name green monkey. The other said this was nonsense. The part in question is in fact unmistakably blue.

We left for Lake Rudolf on the day that the plane arrived to take Doc back to Addis on the first leg of his journey home to Montana. When did we expect to be starting back to Addis, he asked, as we said goodbye.

'In about three weeks,' I said. 'We've Rudolf and Stefanie to look at yet.'

He regretted not to be able to drive back with us, he said, as he grinned his true feelings, but he'd be thinking of us. With a permanent camp established in the Omo Valley, neither clients nor hunters would have to travel again on the road to Addis until a vehicle needed to be replaced. People and personal effects could be flown in and out. Jean could easily have flown back while Tadessa and I brought the Land-Rover, but this, she considered, was too much like deserting. When the safari was over she was coming with us by road – but it obviously worried her.

The trip to Rudolf was gentle and rather uninspiring. We had to return to Turmé and pick up the track from there. It then ran south-west, mainly through monotonous thornbush steepled with the same tall termite mounds, a reflection of the low rainfall and good building soil. These particular termites (*Macrotermes*) use sand grains as bricks which are cemented into position with a mortar of clay particles moistened with saliva. The material is gathered by the workers from the sub-soil and they carry it up the inside of the mound without having to appear on the surface. All very cryptic. No one seems to know exactly why they build such tall towers since the breeding chambers and fungus gardens are always confined to the base. In regions of higher rainfall or shortage of clay, the mounds wash down anyway and tall spires never arise, they stay mound-shaped and just sprout turrets during the building season. Perhaps the taller mounds give the winged swarms a better start as they launch themselves off to found new colonies. Or it might be something much more obscure like regulation of internal humidity.

Despite as much searching as petrol supplies would allow, we saw relatively little wildlife, nothing which couldn't be seen in greater numbers at Murlé, though it remained to be seen how much seasonal movement took place.

At intervals there were police posts to be passed. At these we always expected delays while papers were examined but never felt sure what sort of reception we were in for. At a place called Fejedge we were waved down a few hundred yards before the village by two un-uniformed police who complained angrily that I didn't pull up quickly enough. Twenty miles further on, at an outpost called Hoddo, we actually had to seek out a policeman to ask about a fork in the track. When we found one he was wrapped in an embroidered tablecloth having a siesta. Still wearing his tablecloth he emerged from his hut, told us about the track and returned straight away to his resting.

The land between Hoddo and the Omo delta can only be described as a dust-bowl in the making. Looking at a desert it is possible to imagine, rightly or wrongly, that it has always been so. Where a history of ill-use by man has caused the degradation, one need not dwell upon it.

North of Lake Rudolf, the evidence stares one in the face. The dried-out stumps of trees still stand, the goats teem over the ground, nibbling at the last vestiges of cover which once protected the earth from the constant wind and burning sun. What little rain there is now mainly falls to waste on lifeless, wind-blown sand.

A little way north of Lake Rudolf there is a car ferry across the Omo. At the other side of the river is the village of Kalam. Out of curiosity we went to see the ferry and encountered two of the Kalam police on our side of the river. Tadessa introduced them at a time when I was discovering that I had a little repair job to do under the Land-Rover.

'These are police from Kalam,' he said simply.

From an uncomfortable position on my back I squinted up through grit-filled eyes. Boots with laces missing, denim trousers, string vests, no hats.

'Well tell them they don't look like policemen.' I felt irritable.

'They are asking to see your papers.'

Pushing my luck, I said I wasn't handing out my papers to everyone who felt like asking for them. If they were police (and I didn't really doubt it for an instant) they would have to prove it. Tadessa translated this rather apologetically, I thought.

'They want to know how long we will be here,' he said next.

For a change we were in no hurry to be off. There were a number of odd jobs to be done and it wasn't a bad spot to have lunch. I told them we wouldn't be moving for a couple of hours.

The police went away and someone paddled them across the river in a canoe. Forty minutes later they came paddling back – all smart and uniformed. I received a good-natured salute, though I will never understand why, and I produced my papers. The police set to contentedly copying out the details on a scrap of paper while we ate our bully-beef and biscuits. We parted on the best of terms.

For the benefit of future travellers I should mention that the car ferry wasn't working. When it is working it is powered by two outboard motors for which the customer is asked to provide twenty litres of petrol.

Our tour of the south-west took in only a cursory look at the Lake Stefanie Rift to the east of Lake Rudolf but it was enough to show that the mysterious Lake Stefanie was worthy of another visit. What we found was a dry, flat lake bed about fifty miles long and twenty miles wide lying between parallel rift walls about 4,000 feet high. The northern half of the rift floor was clothed with open thornbush and obviously hadn't been flooded for a long time. The southern half was bare, dry mud.

It was frustrating not to be able to find out more, but petrol supplies would definitely not permit any further driving which was not in the direction of home. Perhaps it was not as frustrating as it might have been for we were in fact ready for a spell in Addis; for clean-looking water that came out of a tap, for something cool to drink and for fresh food. Even the novelty of opening anonymous cans was wearing a bit thin. The canned foods had lost all their labels as a result of the constant jostling about in the Land-Rover and when you expected baked beans you were just as likely to get stewed apricots.

There were no mechanical disasters on the journey home, only minor setbacks. A brake coupling fractured and all the brake fluid ran out. This left us to face precipitous descents with no brakes. Luckily the broken part led to a front brake. I sealed off the front brake system with a ·22 bullet and refilled the rear system – you can manage quite well with two back brakes.

I suppose if there was a climax to the trip it happened a few miles before Soddu on a level stretch of road with all the treacherous mudbaths and crumbling mountain tracks behind us. There was a large pool in the track which I tried to avoid just in case there should be deep mud. There was, and both offside wheels slid into it. I felt the Land-Rover lurch sideways.

'We're going over,' I cried.

Tadessa was in the offside seat and before he could get his window closed the mud was oozing into his right ear. Jean was in the middle and I, by this time, was scrambling up through the driver's door, or more appropriately the hatch. I hauled Jean up after me and as she struggled over the steering wheel she trod on Tadessa's face, pressing it firmly back into the sludge. It is to his lasting credit that he took it very calmly and cheerfully. He gurgled something about being all right and even had the presence of mind to grab my binoculars which fell down next to him. A crowd of people gathered round holding their heads and tutting and someone went into a prolonged '*abet-abet-abet* . . .' recital which is reserved for pretty dreadful circumstances. Fortunately, the roadside trees which had prevented me from circumventing the pool in the first place could not have been more conveniently placed for winching and our predicament was not nearly so bad as it looked. In an hour and a half we were laughing about it in the hotel at Soddu.

5

Lake Stefanie

It was six months after our first visit to Stefanie that I found the opportunity for another trip in that direction. As it was then the middle of the dry season and the fords were low, we would be able to drive direct from Arba Minch without having to use the dreaded Baco route. Jean was delighted about this and we set off quite merrily, collecting two game-guards by prior arrangement from the outpost at Abiata. We were looking forward to seeing Stefanie again. The valley certainly needed to be investigated in more detail. The national scheme for conservation was to be included in the Government's next five-year plan. It would operate on a regional basis and each region had to be subjected to at least a reconnaissance survey after which the more interesting parts could be given more attention. Lake Stefanie lay in an intriguing and isolated valley in the south-west from where we had virtually no recent information. Was the water fresh or salty? Was it deep? Did it support water birds? We had seen the tracks of Grevy's zebra on that first visit, a scarce animal which we saw all too seldom. Were there resident herds in the Stefanie Rift?

The track, by Ethiopian standards, wasn't bad. About sixty-five miles south of Arba Minch it ran through a village called Conso: a remarkable place in that it was built on a terraced hill. In Ethiopia it is unusual to see any attempt at soil conservation. Steep slopes are traditionally laid bare as if the supply of cultivable land were inexhaustible. At Conso miles of hillside had been properly terraced and sorghum and other crops were being grown above neat, drystone retaining walls. Strange that what was obviously a long-established practice and a splendid example to others had remained so localised.

Beyond Conso the rocky track led us through a seemingly endless succession of valleys and passes until I began to feel that we would reach Stefanie with less petrol to spare than we had the first time. Whenever we had a view ahead it was a view of mountains; rising and falling away into the bluish-green obscurity of the far distance.

We came upon the Stefanie Rift unexpectedly. Suddenly we were looking down into a trough between two mountain ranges. It stretched away southwards; a corridor leading to Kenya. Looking from the northern end it wasn't possible to see the floor of the valley for more than a few miles. Detail dissolved into haze.

A long, gentle descent and we had left behind the cultivated hills, the Galla settlements and the last vestiges of a motor track. The track, we knew, continued westwards across the rift, up the other side and on to Baco via a place with the improbable name of Hammer Koké. It was the way we had gone six months before.

We threaded our way southwards between whitish thickets of *Acacia nubica* bushes. It began to rain, though it wasn't supposed to, and the peculiar stink of the acacias was masked by the smell of freshly damp earth. I don't know what gives *nubica* its odour but it's something in the bark. Further south the sandy soil became heavier and, as the shower continued, stickier. Soon we were ploughing twin furrows and had to stop and make camp.

We had two guards with us, Flamingo Feathers and a much quieter fellow called Igezu who was a devout Christian and started every day with exceedingly lengthy prayers which he uttered standing to attention. Igezu was senior to Flamingo Feathers which meant that he claimed the better tent. Flamingo's tent on this occasion was little more than a bedsheet. He had to erect his camp bed first, then build upon it the fragile contraption of sticks, cloth and string which was his tent. It offered a triangular tunnel about a foot high above the bed for him to crawl into. It was sealed at one end so that to sleep with his head to the opening he had to wriggle into it feet first.

Flamingo always stayed cheerful (his only English word was 'yesgood') and seemed immune to discomfort, but I was glad for his sake that it stopped raining before nightfall and we saw no more rain for the rest of the trip.

That night a lion came prowling around camp. At one point, judging by the grunting, he was only a few yards away. I peered out into the moonlight but nothing moved except an animated bedsheet. Flamingo Feathers had heard the lion too.

Lions are still widespread in Ethiopia, despite relentless persecution, but are much more often heard than seen. They seem generally to have adopted the habits of leopards in order to survive. They often inhabit dense thicket and riverine forest and hunt at night. Undoubtedly they take their toll of domestic stock for in some parts there can be little else for them to eat – unless they turn man-eater.

Next morning we found the tracks of our visitor in the wet earth. He had been a big one and had half circled the tents at about twenty yards. A couple of weeks later, at Abiata, I saw Flamingo Feathers telling the other guards about it. Feet as big as dinner plates it had by then, and it had almost come into the tent.

Shortly after leaving camp we crossed the Sagan River. It is joined by a smaller river, the Waito, before it reaches Lake Stefanie. We were now on the western side of the rift and picked up the track which we had used the last time. It led straight to Arboré, a police post on the Sagan.

I had no wish to visit Arboré but there was no way of avoiding it. On the previous occasion the police had refused to let us pass unless we carried a policeman in our Land-Rover which was already loaded to the roof and beyond. I had handled it badly, lost my temper and got arrested. I was only held prisoner for a few hours but it was a tiresome affair and I didn't want a repeat performance.

We followed fresh tyre marks into Arboré and found a truck parked outside the police post and about twenty armed men sitting about in the shade. I drew alongside and climbed out, beaming fatuously. I was determined to remain calm and pleasant whatever the reception.

This time, we got no reception. An official from the Governor's office in Hammer Koké was travelling to Turmé through the Stefanie Rift. No one seemed to care who we were or what we were doing. No one, that is, except the official. He was genuinely interested. He wished us luck with our investigations but felt bound to tell us that we would be wasting our time looking for a lake. South of Arboré there was only dry mud. Stories of a lake were just rumours. There was no water but it always looked like there was. Only last year two people had been tricked by this and had died out on the mud flats; killed by the heat. We should avoid the mountains too, he warned us, the people there were treacherous. Jean asked what happened to the river. It went underground, he said. He wasn't far wrong.

The policeman who had arrested me wasn't there any more. He had been transferred. There was a younger man in charge now and his main concern was to find a metal washer to mend his radio. I gave him one off a spare spark plug.

The official left before us with his escort crowded in the back of the vehicle and hanging over the sides. It can truly be said that the truck bristled with rifles. It raced away down the rift towards the dry river bed which was the pass through the rift wall to Turmé. North of Arboré we had seen a few oryx, Grant's gazelle and dikdik, but following the speeding armoury, we saw only one panic-stricken warthog.

We made camp about half-way down the valley near the western rift wall where the ground had a gentle slope and the scree spilled out on to the flat valley floor. It looked the sort of place which might harbour scorpions in fair numbers and I turned over a few stones to look. Squatting beneath the first stone was a huge, hairy, spider-like creature with enormous jaws. It was a solifuge; an animal related to spiders but without spinning glands and with other differences, such as a segmented hind-body, to those who care to look closely enough. Under the next stone I found another of the yellow-brown monsters, then another and another. After dark the ground would be running with them.

I recalled being stung by a small scorpion a few months earlier. It had been a painful experience but I decided that I would rather be stung by a small scorpion any day than have a large solifuge up my trouser-leg. Yet none of the *Solifugae* are at all poisonous. Silly and irrational, but there it is. Jean felt similarly, only more so.

'Lot of sollies about here,' I said casually. 'I don't think we'll bother with a camp fire.'

During the night we had three of them in the tent. One ran up the inside of the roof and dropped on to my bed. I felt it thump on to my sleeping-bag and dimly remember in my half sleep beating it to a pulp with a sandal. When morning came a long column of ants was disposing of its last remains.

The *Solifugae* are essentially inhabitants of arid country and all are carnivorous. We most often saw them in Ethiopia by the light of the camp fire. A swiftly-moving shape would catch the eye, there'd be a scramble for the torch and more often than not it would be a solifuge. The thing would stop in the light and raise its first pair of hairy legs like outstretched arms, bending itself upwards, as it were, from the waist. The 'arms' actually function as sensory antennae. Some species have relatively long legs and small bodies but ours were usually the squat, heavy-bodied types spanning four or five inches. They would run between the stones and tussocks, 'arms' outstretched in search of prey. They are extraordinarily voracious and in addition to small invertebrates they will tackle lizards and young mice. One authority records seeing a solifuge running down the wall of a hut with a bat in its jaws! Prey is gnashed to shreds in the spiny jaws while the juices are sucked in through a little beak-like mouth beneath. It comes as no comfort to the faint-hearted to read in the text-books that a special set of spines on the mouth-parts is able to produce a twittering noise.

Much remains to be learned about the life history of the *Solifugae* but in the species which have been studied there is an involved courtship during which the male subdues his female by stroking her. After insemination he leaves hurriedly to avoid being eaten. The female lays eggs, up to two hundred, in a burrow of her own making.

The fauna of the western foothills was similar to that in the north of the valley but we saw, in addition, a few lesser kudu and traces of greater kudu on the higher levels where the ubiquitous olive baboons and klipspringer could also be found. From half-way up the escarpment the water on the far side of the valley was clearly visible. Just south of it a group of rocky islands rose from the dry lake bed; a convenient landmark in an otherwise featureless plain. I took a few compass bearings, made a sketch map and planned to move camp to the eastern rift wall, opposite the islands.

By mid-morning the heat in the valley was intense and as we crossed the open mud flats mirages were in evidence everywhere. Water shimmered and gleamed wherever we looked and the distant, ghostly shapes of ostriches and zebras floated over it on long, wobbly stilts. Sometimes the phantom zebras would vanish along with the water but at other times they were left behind, comfortingly real, galloping over the hard baked mud with little puffs of dust at their heels.

In a way it was strangely unnerving crossing the valley for the first time, like being in a vast natural hall of mirrors but completely silent. We found it impossible to judge distances with any measure of accuracy and this somehow added to the general sense of remoteness which I'm sure we all felt very strongly. Jean kept a careful record of the kilometre readings and a constant check on our petrol supply.

Usually the mirages receded before us without appearing to get any closer but at one point it really looked as though we were driving straight into the water. The rocky islands rose out of a great shining pool and I was heading directly for it. Igezu called out from behind me, he must have thought I had gone mad. 'No water here,' I assured him, having seen it from the escarpment in the cool of the morning. Sure enough it disappeared but not before I had begun to have second thoughts myself.

In all, we saw seventy zebras that day, a few solitaries but mostly in small herds. They were all Grevy's, a species first made known to science in 1882 through an Ethiopian specimen which Emperor Menelik sent live to Paris. Standing fifteen hands and heavily-built they are surely the most impressive of wild horses. We watched them in pure admiration as they drummed across the open flats. At a surprisingly short distance their narrow stripes merge so that the animals appear to be a uniform greyish-brown but seen at close quarters they are beautifully marked. I photographed them by cruising alongside for a short time and leaning out of the window. There was no need to steer the Land-Rover nor even to look where I was going – there wasn't a bump or an obstacle in sight.

Watching wild animals we were often disturbed to see how vulnerable they are. An unscrupulous man in a motor car could shoot the Lake Stefanie zebras like so many babies. Merely to chase them hard for prolonged periods could easily kill them by causing a physiological failure.

It was difficult to see what these zebras were living on, for they were mostly observed on the open flats where there was no vegetation at all. Much could have been learnt from an examination of the dung but this requires laboratory facilities which we did not possess. Towards the edges of the flats and especially to the west of the water there were dense, dry beds of *Sporobolus robustus* – coarse tussock grass up to eight feet tall and generally considered to be unpalatable to animals. Much of it had in any case been burnt and only the stalks were left. There were, to be sure, some patches of a much smaller and more acceptable related grass (*Sporobolus spicatus*) and this at least showed signs of having been grazed. We saw very few zebra on the footslopes where better pasture could be found and where oryx and Grant's gazelle were frequently seen grazing. Whatever the diet of the Lake Stefanie zebras, it obviously kept them in superb condition.

Our camp on the east side of the rift was much the same as the one we had left on the west side. Scree, thornbush, *Solifugae* and stifling heat. We would have given a lot for a stiff breeze or a cool dip, but any ideas we may have had about swimming in Lake Stefanie were dispelled very firmly when we got to the waterside: the lake was only ankle-deep; a muddy puddle ten miles across.

We started wading in shallow water between green clumps of

the tall *Sporobolus* and reedmace which we thought marked the lake margin and behind which storks and egrets disappeared like actors into the wings of a stage. We paddled on hopefully, expectantly; this was Lake Stefanie, the secret lake in the hidden valley of southern Ethiopia.

It was clear now why there were such conflicting reports about the lake. The valley floor was so flat that a slight rise or fall of the water level would affect a huge surface area. It might even double or treble its size overnight. From a passing aeroplane it could appear to be a large lake, a swamp, or you might miss it altogether.

After two hours of wading the water wasn't much deeper but we were emerging from the mosaic of clumps and clearings. There was open water now – and it looked solid with flamingoes.

They were mostly lesser flamingoes, hundreds of thousands of them. They formed a crescent of living colour perhaps two miles long. It was impossible to judge the width of the crescent from our angle of view but I doubt it was much less than a quarter of a mile in the centre. When flamingoes are packed so tightly only the individuals around the edges are able to fly; the centre ones have to wait until last before they can spread their wings. We kept our distance and left our flamingoes undisturbed.

It would have been particularly exciting to find the flamingoes nesting but there was no sign of it. This is not to say they never do nest on Stefanie. Flamingoes' nests are merely little mounds of mud with a depression on top – hardly permanent structures in a seasonally fluctuating lake. But it is possible that the marabou storks, of which there were plentiful numbers about, would preclude successful nesting. Leslie Brown's observations on Lake Elmenteita in Kenya revealed that marabous can cause havoc among nesting flamingoes. While stalking about the colony the marabous keep hundreds of thousands of parent flamingoes off their nests and so cause the destruction of many more eggs and chicks than they actually eat.

Lesser flamingoes in such numbers indicate brackish water for they feed mainly upon a lowly group of plants called the *Cyanophyceae*, the blue-green algae, and this thrives particularly in the shallows of soda lakes, as at Abiata. The two *Sporobolus* grasses are also generally taken to indicate saline conditions but to me the water of Stefanie tasted fresh. Later analysis showed that it was indeed slightly saline. Perhaps I was suffering from salt depletion when I drank it.

As we paddled back to where we had left the Land-Rover, we searched the mud for snails to fulfil a request from the British Museum. At one point Jean called me over to where she was snail-grubbing for she had found a strange track across the mud. It was a smooth, broad, winding stripe as if someone had been dragging a heavy sack. It could only have been made by a python and from the width of the impression it had either recently swallowed a very large meal or it had been a phenomenally big snake. We followed the track to where it disappeared into a dense belt of vegetation and I poked and peered tentatively about the edges. That was as far as my courage would take me however and we never discovered how big that python really was.

There were two tiang near the Land-Rover when we got back, a mother and calf. They were the only tiang we ever saw in the Stefanie Rift.

That evening Jean made another discovery. She found a waterhole about half a mile from camp. It was just a muddy hollow in the bed of an otherwise dry creek and warthogs had been wallowing in it. The water felt cool and the hole was big enough to sit in. We sat in it, chucking murky water over each other in sheer delight.

A few days later we found more water – this time among the rocky islands. There were hot springs there and a depression in the rocks held the water in a deep dark pool. Like all the hot springs I have tasted, it was sulphurous but potable. Nearby we found the first signs of human activity which we had seen for several days.

These were a number of stone walls about four feet high and in the form of circles two or three yards in diameter. Near the top of each wall, regularly spaced, slits and holes had been left between the stones.

'Poachers,' I declared, for it seemed obvious to me that the hides had been built for shooting game. Anything which came within range would be easy to shoot for there was no cover around the islands. Igezu looked serious and said something to Flamingo Feathers who nodded in reply. With a combination of mime and Amharic they explained to me that the circles were to protect the marksmen from return fire. There had been a battle here, they said. Men had taken cover among the rocks and built these defences.

Whatever the true interpretation there was no doubt that the stone hides could be very useful to poachers and it remained my view that they had originally been built for that purpose. The day after, however, I had cause to wonder if the guards had not been right.

I was hiking along the hills just south of the camp when I saw a line of men filing past below. There were eight of them and they were heading straight for our camp. Through the binoculars I could see that they carried rifles. I scrambled down the slopes and managed to reach them before they got to camp but there was no way of heading them off. They showed no surprise at seeing a lone *farenge* descend from some of the loneliest hills in Ethiopia. They clearly knew we were there.

I greeted them like old friends but they returned my salaams with stony faces and continued marching towards the camp in single file and in silence. They were the most motley collection of brigands I ever saw in Ethiopia. They were certainly not of the same tribe. One was as light-skinned as any Amhara while the others were much darker but in varying degrees. Their dress was equally assorted but they all carried military-type water bottles, rifles, bandoliers and knives.

As we trooped into camp I felt, to say the least, very apprehensive. I think it was their purposive silent manner which frightened me most. I had become accustomed to primitive tribesmen being armed to the teeth, but not behaving like this: not marching straight for our camp in single file without speaking.

If I read the situation wrongly, so did we all for as the guards appeared and Jean emerged from the tent all three faces took on an expression of frank dismay.

'Visitors,' I announced brightly in Jean's direction. 'For Chrissake hand some biscuits round or something and let's try to look cheerful.'

They were not interested in biscuits. Two of them walked on through the camp and stationed themselves as lookouts on the hills above. A third inspected the Land-Rover. The rest just stood around us. Igezu and Flamingo were both steady, reliable men; they kept their rifles out of sight.

I made a show of checking the time and dumped the field radio on to the bonnet of the Land-Rover. There would be no chance of using it until 9.00 hours next morning but it might look impressive. I switched on and got the usual whistles, snatches of morse and other interference. I muttered some nonsense into the microphone and clapped it to my ear as if listening to replies. Jean scanned the sky to the north as though she expected to see an aeroplane.

Our visitors withdrew a few yards to confer, whispering and pointing to the Land-Rover. The lookouts stayed at their posts above us. There was nothing we could do. Jean pottered around the tent, tidying and fiddling about with nothing in particular. I mechanically turned the pages of the newspapers from the plant press. The guards sat outside their tents, doodling in the dust with bits of twig.

It was a tense time and it seemed a long time for it was abundantly clear that our fate was being decided. Behind me in the tent was a ·30-06 rifle with four rounds of ammunition in the magazine. The guards each had a ·303 beneath their beds. There wasn't much comfort in this.

Needless to say we were not murdered but the amazing thing is – we were not even robbed. After ninety minutes the company decided to leave – each munching a biscuit. I don't think any of us got much sleep that night. Igezu prayed longer and harder than I ever heard him pray before, though he equalled his performance again at dawn next morning.

One problem which had been bothering us throughout the trip was what happened to the river. The Waito and Sagan Rivers together produced a considerable flow of water; more water, I reckoned, than could be accounted for by evaporation from the lake. It must be going somewhere. From the top of the escarpment it was possible to distinguish an extensive green area at the northern end of the lake. We decided this was worth exploring before we left the valley. The guards packed up camp with alacrity and we set out to skirt the lake on the western side until we reached the northern limit.

The green turned out to be a vast meadow of low-growing sedge where the river was lost in a swampy expanse of interconnected pools and channels. Most of the water appeared to soak away and evaporate in this region without ever reaching the open water of the lake.

I took the Land-Rover as far on to the sedge marsh as I dared, which I suppose was about a mile. Beyond this the ground was too wet for safe driving so we walked. When we later came to drive off the marsh the depression made by the tyres had in one place begun to fill with water. I steered to one side to put the wheels on to new ground – and went straight up to the axles in a soft patch.

We set to with spades and shovels but quickly realised that digging would do no good at all. Beneath the surface of leaves and roots there was a sticky wet layer of black humified clay. Holes rapidly filled with water. The Land-Rover needed to be pulled or lifted on to the surface again. The nearest trees were miles away and there wasn't even a log anywhere to use as a 'dead man' for the winch. Trying to jack up the vehicle only forced the jack into the ground. We stood the jack on the shovel; that disappeared too.

A few yards in front of the Land-Rover there was a relatively dry patch and I set the guards to digging a deep trench at right angles to the Land-Rover with a narrow slit for the cable running down to the bottom of the trench. I began to remove the Land-Rover bumper to use as a 'dead man'. It seemed a good idea; we all thought so.

When the winch was set up, Flamingo Feathers took the lever. There were a few moments of creaking strain and the wheels began to move. We shouted encouragement as Flamingo threw his weight against the lever. The bumper crumpled in the middle, folded itself into a V and was dragged through the clay like a ploughshare. The Land-Rover slumped back into its bed. It was during the ensuing pause for breath and headscratching that someone noticed that we were about to have company – again.

Tiny figures could just be made out. They were moving towards us from the western escarpment. Standing on the roof of the Land-Rover and squinting through binoculars, Jean began counting them.

'Thirty. And they've all got guns,' she added, as they drew closer.

For several minutes we stood with feelings oddly alternating between anxiety and rejoicing. The timely arrival of so much man-power was unbelievable good fortune. Or was it trouble? In the end it proved to be neither.

Feelings crystallised as the men came into view. Mainly they were fine physical specimens, very dark and naked. Some had their legs daubed with white. They carried folded blankets over their shoulders. The majority had rifles, a few had only spears or sticks. I knew at once who they were. They were the terror of the lower Omo, the feared 'Marrile' of the Kenya border. They were warriors of the Hammer tribe.

As we shook hands with the first half dozen or so to reach us it was clear that they meant us no harm. They were just intensely curious. They crowded round the Land-Rover, peering through the windows and jostling each other to see their own reflection in the glass. They obviously took a great pride in their appearance for they wore necklaces and bracelets and their hair styles were most elaborate. The whole of their hair was plastered and patterned with brightly coloured clays. Feather plumes had been worked into the clay before it had set hard. The technique is widespread in south-west Ethiopia and also, I believe, among the Turkana of north-eastern Kenya but I had never before seen it so consistently well done.

A few of the warriors took the cloths from their shoulders and wrapped them around their waists, tucking them beneath their bandoliers. The rest of the group followed suit. I was intrigued by the bandoliers and ammunition pouches. They were professionally made and looked brand-new. All were very well filled. I was told some weeks later in Addis that Hammer tribesmen had fairly recently ambushed some soldiers from Baco and had taken all their weapons and ammunition.

Curiosity satisfied, the warriors began to sit around us on their little carved stools. The various tribes of the region all make these stools in exactly the same design. They are cut from one piece of very light wood and constitute the only furniture the nomads possess. They are used both as a stool and a head rest. The men carry them, together with their weapons, wherever they go.

One of Flamingo Feathers' most valuable qualities was his ability to make himself understood in a variety of Galla tongues. He had one language in common, it appeared, with two of the nomads. I made signs of pushing the Land-Rover and indicated to Flamingo to get the men to help. They were not enthusiastic; perhaps because it was too much like coolie work. Nevertheless he persuaded about fifteen of them to assist and he made a gallant job trying to co-ordinate their efforts. It was hopeless. They pushed in all directions and seemed to be determined to put most of their weight against the windows.

I tried them pulling, like a tug-o'-war team, on the cable. No effect. Next I stood the now V-shaped bumper in the trench, placed the spare wheel behind it, fixed the cable and started winching again. Slowly the side of the trench caved in as the soft clay welled up in front. The bumper and the wheel began to slide almost imperceptibly upwards.

'Get them to stand on it,' I yelled, but the nomads were losing interest. Many of them had wandered off to bathe in the pools nearby.

A few men were eventually mustered and there was a final all-out effort with the tyres at half pressure, Flamingo and Igezu on the winch, myself trying everything I knew from the driver's seat and Jean and half a dozen warriors huddled together on the bumper and spare wheel. They all fell off when the assemblage burst through the side of the trench and slithered upon the surface. With more presence of mind I could have secured a photograph which would have been the pride of my collection.

It sounds hard to believe that thirty-three men with a winch couldn't pull a Land-Rover out of the mud. But we couldn't. The sun was setting and the Hammer were drifting away back to their *tukuls* on the escarpment. Tomorrow they had agreed to bring us a very large tree trunk. But that was tomorrow. We prepared to spend the night on the marsh.

It had been oven-hot all day and throughout the winching, digging and heaving there had scarcely been a time when one or other of us hadn't been gulping at the hot spring water with which we had last filled the jerry cans. Now we started on the water from the swamp pools. Two pints of sedgy tea and we collapsed beneath the essential mosquito nets and slept.

We drove off the marsh the following evening. It was done by breaking up a safari box and using the boards to make a large platform for the jack. We then carried loads of dry grass stalks from about a mile away to fill the holes beneath the wheels. On to the bed of straw we packed dry earth, which stayed dry. We had to do this with each wheel in turn and it took all day.

We decided on the method early in the morning and started work on it straight away without waiting to try with the tree trunk. In retrospect this was wise for when the 'tree trunk' arrived, at about noon, it was being carried in one hand by one of the more youthful warriors!

That evening we made camp on a firm, high bank of the Sagan River and we spent the next day idling about while Flamingo Feathers lost all my fish hooks one by one in an unsuccessful attempt to catch a free supper. The relaxation was bliss and with the confidence of knowing that we had enough petrol, the journey home, by the way we had come, was a pleasure.

6

The Far West

The week before Christmas is not the best time to embark on a month's safari to some malarial swamp near the Sudan border. Nobody wants to come.

Since leaving Lake Stefanie I had spent just one week in Addis; long enough to catch a foul cold (though the weather was glorious) and get thoroughly fed up with the place. It had been taxation time for the Land-Rover. Two days of gathering signatures, sticking revenue stamps and paying fees. I was all for getting away. Anywhere would do but Gambella *Awraja* fitted best into our overall fieldwork programme.

Ethiopia was then divided administratively into fourteen provinces each under the control of a Governor-General whose authority devolved through the governors of the provincial sub-districts – *Awrajas* at the first level, then smaller districts called *Weredas*. The most westerly *Awraja* is Gambella in the province of Illubabor. A mass of land, subject to regular and extensive flooding, thrusts westwards into the Sudan between rivers which there form the Ethiopian boundary.

Had it been only one week to everybody's Christmas I might have been persuaded to wait, but the Ethiopians celebrate theirs on 7 January and this is followed twelve days later by the Feast of the Epiphany (*Timkat*) which no Ethiopian wants to miss. So on 19 December I found myself bowling impatiently westwards with a bottle of aspirins and only one companion. Berhanu (yes, the one who came with us on that first trip to Nachisar) said he didn't mind being away for Christmas but would quite like to be back for *Timkat*. Jean had pleasanter things to do for Christmas and we decided that she should do them. Afterwards she would fly to Gambella to join us.

It was a good road westwards, tarmac for a start then gravel.

Three hours from Addis we were rattling over a steel bridge which spans the Omo River. Here the river is called the Gibbe and it hurries along noisily in a bouldery bed. There is pleasant scenery in the Gibbe Valley, dissected hillsides and steep slopes dotted with *Combretum* bushes reaching down to the river. A welcome change from the plateau with its endless hamlets and plots of false bananas (*Ensete ventricosa*).

The indigenous *Ensete*, along with the eucalyptus trees which Menelik introduced, are everywhere cultivated on the Ethiopian Plateau. They are an integral feature of the rural scene, like *tukuls* and tin roofs. No one who has been to Addis Ababa and travelled into the surrounding countryside could adequately describe what he saw without reference to the groves of eucalyptus and clusters of false bananas whose giant leaves, two or three yards long, sprout up from a common base like turnip-tops. The leaf blades tend to split down to the midrib and hang in tattered sections which are used as disposable dinner plates and sheets of wrapping paper. String and matting can be made from the fibres of the midrib. We were passing through Guraghe country and the Guraghe people make even more use of *Ensete* than do the Amharas. They grind up the leaf-bases to make flour for bread.

The Guraghe are interesting people though they are not visibly very different from their neighbours. During the fourteenth century, we are told, invaders from the north of Ethiopia settled among the people in and around the Gibbe Valley and today's half million Guraghes are their descendants, now speaking their own language. Their homelands are still to the south and west of Addis but the Guraghe come to the capital to work, often as hawkers and merchants, in which capacity their business acumen has earned them quite a reputation.

We passed through Jimma in the late afternoon. The town is the capital of Kaffa province, once a Muslim kingdom but brought within the boundaries of modern Ethiopia by Menelik during the last century. The people are still Mohammedans. Jimma lies on the eastern edge of a vast forest. Despite all their efforts to destroy it by felling, burning and cultivating, the people of highland Kaffa and Illubabor still possess the finest forest in the Empire. They have evolved a cottage industry from wood: Jimma stools, heavy three-legged stools crudely carved in one piece from solid sections of tree trunk and sold at the roadside for less than a pound. In Addis they sell for several times the price.

Our track ran through coffee plantations and a roadworking clangour of mechanical shovels, bulldozers and tractors. Kaffa and Illubabor produce most of Ethiopia's coffee and coffee forms more than half of the nation's total exports, hence the importance of a road. The hoardings announced that an Italian firm was doing the job and America was paying for it.

Finding a camp site was a problem. There was a constant stream of people along the road and absolutely nowhere that we could pull off to be quiet. It was well after dark when we finally crawled into our tents at the roadside. Things weren't much better the next day, though we soon left the road behind and found ourselves on a relatively peaceful forest track, but even here we were either on a slope, up on one side, down on the other; or else in a cutting between earth banks so it was still impossible to pull off to the side.

I believe that track through the forest was the only place I ever saw colobus monkeys, in any numbers, on the ground. They bounded along the banks like enormous black and white squirrels. In the more open areas the trees were entwined with a climbing plant (*Combretum paniculatum*) which was heavy with brilliant scarlet flowers. The woods rang with the loud raucous calls of silvery-cheeked hornbills and in the clearings we watched the dipping flight of these remarkable pied birds. The female, if she nests every year, must spend a third of her life imprisoned with her eggs and young in a hollow tree. Like other hornbills she walls herself in with mud brought to the nest by the male. He then has to feed her, mainly on fruits, through a slit in the wall.

We found a reasonable camp site just before Goré, a village through which we drove the following morning. The streets of Goré were cobbled with jagged rocks set upright like broken glass along a prison wall. They were ruinous to tyres but in wet weather, I imagine, the inhabitants of Goré could walk on the points and keep their feet dry. The houses were raised on stone-walled terraces on either side of the street. Altogether Goré was singularly well prepared for heavy rain. With sixty inches a year, it needed to be.

Beyond Goré we left the plateau and the rain forest at about five and a half thousand feet and began a steep, winding descent through open broadleaf savanna-woodland to the flood plains of the Baro River. The leaves of the *Terminalia* and *Combretum* trees which dominated the woodland were turning yellow-brown and many had already fallen. Tall, tawny grass fringed the blackened clearings where fire had passed a day or two before.

It was strangely deserted country now; no more settlements, no people, no stock. This was partly explained by the swarms of tsetse fly. At any one time we could count a hundred or more sitting on the wings of the Land-Rover and pattering at the windows. But there was also an absence of wildlife. Birds were relatively few and the only mammals we saw were a bush duiker and a warthog. At that time of the year the western lowlands would be more or less like this for hundreds of miles, weeks of overland travelling. Everywhere the lush woodlands of the wetter west spend the dry season in the way that temperate woodlands pass the winter, but the falling leaves show none of the splendour of a fine autumn. There is no deep and colourful carpet beneath the trees and it would not last long if there were. The drab leaves fall to earth as food for the termites, which after dark teem beneath the litter with an audible rustling; or as fuel for the fires which sweep through the long grass. Throughout the year, through the wet and dry, the cycles of nature turn more swiftly in the tropics.

Half-way down the descent we met the River Baro in its upper reaches. It was crossed by a Bailey bridge and nearby there was a level place to pitch the tent; we stopped, though it was early. At the other side of the river the gorge was ablaze and the air was filled with floating, sooty fragments of grass. At the top of the gorge an Abyssinian roller patrolled the edge of the flames, fanning brilliant sky-blue wings as he alighted momentarily to seize a fleeing insect. The burning was deliberate. It was someone's job to keep the track open by burning the grass each year. There were two of them at it, we passed them the next day, very black fellows wearing only loin cloths and each carrying a small sack of food and matches. They had spent the night in a shelter of twigs and grass which was now being consumed by their after-breakfast arson. Thereafter we had to push our way, in places, through roof-high grass.

The many streams and dry gullies had all been properly bridged at one time. The brick-built abutments still stood but the bridges had gone and the deep drops were now only spanned by logs and branches – the gaps sometimes covered with flattened oil-drums. In view of the fact that ours was positively the first vehicle to travel the road since the last dry season I was highly suspicious about the bridges. Termites can do an awful lot in half a year.

Before midday we were on flat ground at a little over 2,000 feet. At noon we rounded a bend in the track and we saw the Baro again; now quite unrecognisable, a much wider, slower river. On the far side there were people washing, fishing and fiddling with boats. It was the township of Gambella.

The Baro is the largest in volume of the three main rivers which drain through the Gambella swamplands. Further south there is the Gilo and, south of that, the Akobo. The water of all three flows eventually into the White Nile. Our plan was to drive southwards as far as the Gilo, leave the Land-Rover there and go into the country between the Gilo and Akobo with porters. I hoped to get this part of the trip finished by the beginning of January then return to the town of Gambella to meet Jean off the plane from Addis. She would join us for the latter part of the survey north of the Gilo.

In Gambella there was a man called Philip who was retained by the Wildlife Department as a game-guard. He was said to be a local man who ought to be useful as a guide and interpreter. It seemed worth trying to locate him since we had to visit the town anyway to buy petrol.

We were ferried across the Baro in a large dugout canoe. The ferryman was a very tall black spindly fellow, a Nilotic negro of the Anuak tribe which is one of the two main tribes of Gambella, the other being the Nuer. Traditionally the Anuak live by cultivating the levees of the rivers and streams. They generally keep no livestock apart from chickens. The Nuer are cattle-men whose homeland extends westwards into the Sudan and on towards the Nile. In the town the Nuer were easily distinguished by the rows of tribal scars across their foreheads.

Berhanu went off to enquire about the game-guard while I sought out the shops. There were three extraordinarily general stores each kept by a Greek. I went to one kept by Nicolas who was patiently watching a group of Nuer customers sorting through a box of buttons; a few miles further west they hadn't got round to bothering about clothes, with or without buttons. I bought some bread, wire gauze, a few other odd items and asked about petrol. He had that too but it was kept at the warehouse. We left the Nuer to their button-sorting under the supervision of Nicolas's shop assistant and strolled off to the warehouse.

Nicolas had been in Gambella for forty years, he told me. He seemed more resigned to it than contented. The town was built by the British about seventy years ago as a trading post, it being about as far upriver as the steamboats could pass from the Sudan. Ethiopian produce, notably ivory, was brought from Goré by the road we used. Although no longer a trading post, the history of the town can be read in the brick-built wharfs and warehouses (Nicolas's was one), the tree-lined streets and the colonial-type bungalows. Nicolas had one of these too.

Berhanu turned up at the warehouse, having drawn a blank in his man-hunt. We tramped back to the Land-Rover with two jerry cans of petrol and spent the rest of the afternoon by the river, fitting gauze-covered frames into the Land-Rover windows. I believed it should be possible to drive about without sweltering to death behind closed windows or being exsanguinated by tsetse flies. While we worked, a giant kingfisher the size of a pigeon perched on a branch determinedly thrashing a fish into insensibility. I remember it from among dozens of more common birds which frequented the river – herons, egrets, hammerkops and so on. One might encounter the same sort of birds on suitable waters all the way to the Cape. For some creatures a river is not a barrier but a sort of highway home, cutting through deserts, swamps and forests alike and enabling water birds to live in very varied country and distribute themselves about the continent more widely than just about any other avian group.

The hammerkop, while I'm on the subject, is worth a mention if you have never had the chance to see it. It is about the size of a big crow, brown all over, with a heavy bill and the back of its head projecting in a tuft of feathers which produces the hammer-headed look in profile. It builds a nest of enormous proportions, made of sticks and almost always in a tree. It flies rather like an owl and feeds largely on frogs and tadpoles which it brings to light by paddling and shuffling its feet in the mud. It is an active bird by day and is said to carry on being active well into the night. It belongs to a family all of its own – the *Scopidae*. Aesop might have made much of the hammerkop had it been a more familiar bird.

The following morning Berhanu went off early to have another go at finding the game-guard. This time he succeeded in winkling him out and brought him to see me. He was an Anuak with a goatee beard and protruding front teeth. He arrived complaining that the last time he had ventured outside the town he had received no *per diem* allowance. I paid him some in advance and we got away without too much delay.

The rains, I was told, had gone on a little longer than usual that year so the grass was still green. The important thing about this was that the people hadn't been able to burn it. Visibility was nil as we pushed through the eight-foot-high stalks of *Panicum* and *Hyparrhenia* grass. Had the black clay still been wet we should have been unable to make any headway at all.

After two or three hours we arrived at the Chiru River, a tributary of the Gilo. There was an Anuak village there called Chiobo and everyone came running to watch the first motor of the season fording the river. Children ran and splashed in front of the wheels while mothers with babes in arms yelled from the banks. I noticed that the young women wore sections of elephant tusks bored out as armlets and some carried gourds with patterns and figures carved into them. Philip and the village headman greeted each other like brothers and I was told that the headman had much information about wild animals. It sounded to me like any excuse for hanging around the village but I couldn't afford not to hear what the old man had to say. Local information is anything but reliable but it sometimes turns out to be true.

There was a very good place, he told us, not far away. Tomorrow he would take us there.

'Why not today?' I asked.

He explained that first we must all go to the next village to report to the police, otherwise when they heard he had been helping the *farenge*, they would think he was involved in some secret deal. I had to admit that he was probably right. The police palaver went off fairly well and the headman gave us a guide the day after to take us to the Good Place.

We drove over better-drained land in open savanna where the grass had dried and been burnt. It was a pleasure to be able to look around again, even at a temporarily blackened and rather grim landscape. The unbroken patterns of branches and twigs lay raised in grey ash on the ground where they had burnt. Thick stalks of the bigger grasses poked up like burnt canes, ringed in black where the leaves had been. The scattered trees had dropped their leaves. Mostly they were *Combretum* and *Terminalia* and one called *Piliostigma* which has a leaf shaped like a camel's foot; nondescript trees but tolerant of annual fires. Quite frequently there would be a *Stereospermum* brightening the charred scene with panicles of fragrant pink trumpets or a *Lonchocarpus* with showers of purplish blooms. There were gardenias too, in plenty, but they were not in flower.

The Good Place proved to be a marshy depression, a shallow flood plain, bright green with grasses and sedge and bordered with clumps of borassus palms which bore clusters of yellow fruits the size of coconuts but hopelessly out of reach. In South Africa the flood plain would be called a vlei, in other parts of southern Africa – a *dambo*. Gambella is a mass of vleis; this one just happened to be easily accessible but at that time it was also far enough away from any other water to be used as a regular watering place by game. A pair of bohor reedbuck bounded away as we approached, defassa waterbuck fled in a panic which told its own story, and we found a number of very recent buffalo tracks though the animals evaded us. I made a mental note of a comfortable-looking camp site for a future occasion and we took our guide back to Chiobo.

We pressed on south, crossing another Gilo tributary and passing through Abobo where we had already made our peace with the law. Beyond Abobo the tree cover thickened and soon we were driving through forest no less dense than the rain forest which we had left behind at the edge of the plateau. I later determined from the air that this belt of lowland forest was in fact continuous with the rain forest of the plateau but it had not been so in the vicinity of the road. We edged past the buttresses of *Celtis* trees which towered 100 feet above us and occasionally passed massive trunks of trees which rose half as high again. There were a few halts while we cut through lianas or dragged fallen logs aside but the track was generally good and we made excellent progress. Unfortunately, the gauze screens at the windows didn't last long for the branches tore them out. The tsetse flies came in in strength and Philip had a mild form of hysteria. Berhanu remained stoical as ever.

I was intrigued at one point by a signpost written in English and nailed to a tree. It said 'GOG'. It had gone on to say something about a clinic but half of it was broken off. Minutes later we reached a village: it was Gog. Gog-in-the-forest, the forest of Gog. With a name like that there ought to be dragons. I drove speedily through Gog staring straight ahead and pretending not to notice anyone; I was quite determined not to be waylaid and forced to spend another night near squawking chickens, barking dogs and screaming babies. We passed a party of travellers on the track, some of them dumped their bundles down to wave. 'Masenga tribe,' said Philip, 'the little people of the forest.' I suppose by comparison with the Nilotic men, they were little people.

The forest began to peter out and we were plunged once more into tall grass; taller, if anything, than before. Someone had gone through on foot and left a just-discernible path. It led in the right direction according to the compass so we followed it, thumping into concealed tree stumps, bouncing in and out of elephants' foot-holes and stopping, at infuriatingly short intervals, to clear piles of grass seeds and debris from the boiling radiator.

At 6 p.m. we burst into a clearing which proved to be the airstrip on an American Mission Station. It was on the banks of the Gilo River.

Berhanu and Philip went to spend the night in an Anuak hut near the mission. The missionaries were not at home. I camped by the river. It rained during the night, unseasonally, as it so often did. A toad came ashore and settled somewhere under the head end of my groundsheet. It gave vent to lusty bursts of croaking whenever I dozed off. Perhaps I prompted it by snoring but I don't think so. The toad revealed one of the very few disadvantages of a stitched-in groundsheet. I couldn't bring myself to silence it, with a boot from the inside, and to evict it I should have had to crawl out into the wet grass and fish about under the tent. I lay there listening to the rain and wondering what tomorrow would bring.

One of the main reasons for wanting to go south of the Gilo was to investigate the status of the Nile lechwe, a swamp-dwelling animal which together with another medium-sized antelope, the white-eared kob, is found only in the Gambella area and the southern Sudan. Within this range the kob undertake seasonal migrations *en masse* and would be easier to see another time. They are merely a colour variation of a fairly common species anyway. But the lechwe were reported to be concentrated in a few permanent swamps south of the Gilo and they are a species quite distinct from their nearest lechwe relatives which live some 2,000 miles further south. Not that the lechwes are a particularly unique group; in fact all the kobs and lechwes are pretty close relatives and have been lumped with the waterbuck in the genus *Kobus*. To prove the point there is a triple hybrid on record whose parents were a kob and a Nile lechwe-waterbuck cross! The distinctive thing about the Nile lechwe is the colour. The females are a light chestnut while the old males are almost black with a large white saddle across the shoulders. There are other white markings on the face and limbs and their ringed horns slope backwards in a smooth S-shaped curve. All very striking. I had never seen one. I still haven't.

We found next morning that the Gilo could be forded on foot, being only waist-deep. Since the mission was also used as a crocodile hunters' base the danger from crocodiles was negligible. I told myself this, reassuringly, as we waded across. A year or two before, an American Peace Corps worker doing much the same thing had been seized by a crocodile at Gambella. Karl Luthy, the Swiss hunter who had set up the camp on the Omo, was there at the time and shot the suspected killer. The young man's body, in large recognisable portions, was then recovered from the animal's stomach. I had seen the photographs.

We thrust ourselves through the grass and rushes of the far side in stifling humidity and something gave me a kind of nettle-rash. Philip was useful here for he knew that there was a settlement within a short distance at which we could enquire about tracks. Floundering blindly on, smarting and sneezing, we reached the place and enquired. There were no tracks. Nor did there appear to be any need for them. The Anuak community kept chickens and grew and stored enough grain for their needs. Bananas grew around their huts. A narrow footpath (tunnel would be a better word) to the river was the only track they had to maintain.

I climbed a tree and looked around over a calm sea of grass. Not an open area in sight. It seemed pointless to push further south without having any idea where we were pushing to. I gave up and we worked our way back to the Land-Rover.

We drove further west along the Gilo to try to cross the river lower down. We skirted Lake Tata which B. H. Jessen described in 1906. There wasn't much game about then according to Jessen. There was even less now. He mentioned the shooting of two giraffes, a couple of elephants and a bushbuck. Giraffe still survive in Gambella but I only saw them from the air.

Both Nuer and Anuak tribesmen take to hunting during the dry season. Using snares and shooting from pit-hides near water holes, they take a very heavy toll. Though I didn't predict it at the time, the slaughter was to get much worse. Gambella was then accommodating large numbers of refugees from the southern Sudan, and when the civil war there ended about three years later, firearms and ammunition were to spare in greater numbers than ever before.

We left the riverside and drove once again across a fired landscape where that morning a small herd of elephants had left perfect footprints in the ash. A soot-smudged lelwel hartebeest stared lugubriously for a moment before cantering off; swallow-tailed bee-eaters balanced on a trembling twig, a Denham's bustard hurried away, glancing nervously this way and that. You could see things when the grass had been burnt.

Grass burning in Africa as a land-management practice is a highly controversial subject. The effect of fire on soil and vegetation can be complex and far-reaching; sometimes beneficial in one way and destructive in another. Moreover, research findings from experiments in one locality need to be applied with great caution in a similar situation elsewhere for so many variables are involved. In Gambella the annual burning of flood-plain grasses does not, I would guess, do any harm, and it certainly makes life more pleasant.

We encountered the river again at a place called Abol. Like all the Anuak settlements it was just a tight little cluster of thatched *tukuls*. The people of Abol knew the lechwe swamps to the south and I asked Philip to try to hire a guide and porters. He spoke to the village headman, without much apparent enthusiasm, in the Anuak tongue as they sipped at a brew which I did not sample. Berhanu drank his in silence. Naked, pot-bellied children who were romping with the poultry found *farenge*-watching more engaging and they came to sit and lie in the dust around me, gazing and giggling. The older girls and women, clutching the eternal babes-in-arms, stood back to stare more politely and I in turn found a certain fascination in watching one of them abstractedly sucking a little ivory peg in and out through a hole in her lower lip. Among the negroes of the Nile it was easy to forget that one was still in Haile Selassie's Empire.

The chief shook his head as he finished talking and put down his glass.

'No one will accompany us.' Philip interpreted in his excellent mission-taught English. 'In one more month, yes, then it will be easy, but while the grass is green – impossible.'

I couldn't think of anything else to try. The simple fact was that we had come a month too soon and even if we did get across the Gilo it would almost certainly be a wasted effort. We would see nothing. In other years, late December would probably be late enough, but not this year.

On the way back Philip acquired an enormous branch of bananas which he stowed away in the back of the Land-Rover. Later he asked if I would mind taking back a few things from the American Mission Station. These turned out to be large wooden window frames with glass in, and a tin chest. The chest went inside and the frames were lashed on to the roof-rack. At the next stop, where I had to collect a sack of grain (or did the papayas come next?), I discovered that the sharp edges of the chest had smashed my plastic jerry cans. The chest was promptly relegated to the roof-rack. The day after, in the forest, a low branch drove it through a jar of formalin in which I had a few specimens stored. The formalin dribbled in down the back door and added to the mess which Philip's mashed bananas had produced. I felt like breaking his windows.

There was a slight delay in Gog while I convinced the *Wereda* Governor that I hadn't seen him waving when we hurtled through the village the first time.

Gog, like the rest of Gambella, had suffered a recent outbreak of sleeping sickness and reinforcements of missionaries were moving into the district. Two young Swedes had just crossed the Baro from the town of Gambella when we arrived on the south bank at the end of December. Their vehicle had been ferried across on three dugout canoes and was winched up the near-vertical bank on the south side. The last part of the performance was hard to believe. As there was no convenient tree, an old rear axle had been sunk into the ground like a post and the cable fixed to that. The actual winching was a race to get the vehicle to the top before the axle pulled out. In an attempt to even the odds, one of the ferrymen had a sledgehammer with which he kept battering the old axle down while his mates did the winching. I am certain that our loaded Land-Rover would never have made it.

I took some satisfaction in paying Philip off and dismissing him; his incessant moaning about the tsetse flies had been very tiresome. It was in any case quite unnecessary for him to return with us for a closer look at the forest and the open areas which had been selected during our eight-day recce.

Jean (and more missionaries) arrived safely at the airstrip and we exchanged news, as one does on these occasions, by firing all our broadsides in the first ten seconds and later firing them over again until they had no further discernible impact. More bread was procured, petrol was ferried from Nicolas's warehouse and by evening we felt prepared for an early start. But by nightfall Berhanu had still not appeared at the camp with the last two cans of petrol. Instead, Philip turned up again – with the news that Berhanu had been arrested.

The story was long and involved, but in brief, Berhanu had been a lieutenant in the Imperial Body Guard and had served a six-year prison sentence for his part in the attempted *coup d'état* of 1960. Now, in Gambella, he had been spotted by an old enemy in the police force and jailed on suspicion of being on the run.

It was about this time that Thomas, a Yugoslav hunter, arrived in Gambella from Addis. He had lived in Ethiopia for most of his life and was on good terms with the Gambella police. He generously offered to be Berhanu's guarantor and the police accepted. Berhanu was released on condition that he reported at the police station twice daily. His identity card was retained for verification. This would take time since no telegram or radio messages from Addis were acceptable to the police; only signed and sealed letters. It was an unfortunate place to be stuck, for, on our side of the river, it was a sultry 106° F. in the shade and there wasn't much shade. The insect life, too, was a torment. The mosquitoes were out in force before the tsetse flies had retired for the night. On the second day Jean decided that she should have stayed at home for the New Year.

We sweated it out until some missive or other from Addis moved the police to relax the conditions of Berhanu's parole. He was permitted free movement within Gambella *Awraja*. We hurried away to the vlei beyond Chiobo and camped in the deepest shade we could find.

During the next few days we added tiang, roan antelope and bushpig to our list of game animals in the surrounding countryside. The roan, handsome scimitar-horned antelope were the first I had ever seen but oddly enough the thing I remember most vividly from that period was a small, dusky bird.

I first saw it flying silently over the vlei just after sunset. In the failing light my first impression was that a fairly large bat was being mobbed by two smaller bats which were fluttering along just above and behind it. But in the same instant I realised that I was looking not at a trio of bats but at a single bird. It was a standard-winged nightjar and it was soon joined by another one in its flight back and forth above the marsh. They were both males in breeding plumage and had one primary feather (the ninth) on each wing elongated so that it projected about a foot beyond the wing tip. The web of these display feathers is confined to a terminal 'flag' which flutters along with no apparent connection to the bird since the thin shaft of the feather is usually invisible when the bird is flying. Standard-winged nightjars are intertropical migrants and these males had probably come from the north to breed in the southern part of their range. I called Jean over and we stood watching until the scops owls were calling to each other above the water and we had to leave the scene to better eyes.

We never saw or heard any large predators whilst we were in Gambella. There was one rocky hill within a day's walking distance where traces of leopard would not have been out of place. I walked there but found only baboons which chose not to stay, and a colony of hyrax. I did, however, find a leopard trap. It consisted of a large wooden cage built around stakes driven into the ground. It was open at both ends and the roof was piled with boulders. Anything entering the cage would press against a trigger-stick which was supposed to make the roof crash down on to the victim. I sprung the trap with a branch. Nothing happened. I wiggled the trigger about in simulation of a more co-operative type of animal and the roof duly descended; but it wedged firmly again about two feet from the ground. One might almost approve of traps like that!

Presumably the trap had been built by Anuaks but there were no dwellings for miles. Indeed, I remember that kopje as a rather lonely uninspiring sort of place; a grey landmark seen through a smoky haze where soot and the spoil of termites coated the bark of dingy trees. The smell of bush fire was pervasive and swarms of tiny black sweat bees swam before the eyes against the blur of unfocused twigs and brown-yellow leaves. There was monotony too for the ears, in the pressure-cooker shrilling of cicadas.

It is not always easy to spot a cicada when it sits motionless on the rough bark of a tree. The ones I discovered in Gambella were greyish, like inch-long flies with folded wings and large heads. They are sap-suckers, relatives of aphids, and their loud incessant noise comes not from rubbing but from the incredibly rapid pulsing of a pair of tymbals on the insect's underside, like the tops of two tin-cans bulging in and out 400 times a second. The savannas of Gambella looked, smelt and sounded like fired *miombo*, the broadleaf woodland which clothes most of south-central Africa, but the similarity was only superficial. The species were different.

In the forest where we spent the last few days of our safari it was ten degrees cooler and extremely pleasant. Narina's trogons, most colourful of birds, flashed scarlet between the green leaves and each morning white-crowned robin chats called and whistled above us like tame parrots. Not far away a scaly francolin sat secretly, like a dark partridge, on a clutch of buff-coloured eggs. One bird, a babbler, I decided would have to be collected, as it looked like a completely unrecorded species for Ethiopia.

I think that of all places a still and beautiful forest is the worst setting in which to have to shoot. In a commercial forest with axe-blows ringing and saws screeching it wouldn't matter. But in the church-like atmosphere which exists beneath tall, silent trees one is intensely aware of sounds; the sounds of birds, the scrape of a dry, falling leaf, the snap of a twig. At such a time, pulling a trigger is like an act of vandalism.

I committed my vandalism early one morning with a ·410 shotgun. There was an earth-shattering explosion followed by a little cry. In the tent some thirty yards away, Jean had rammed a nailfile into her finger! I got my babbler which in the end turned out to be a common white-rumped babbler without a white rump.

There was plenty of interest in the forest and our note-books were crammed and the plant presses bulged when, in mid-January, we arrived once again at the Baro River. The police had received no news, they said. They could not permit us to leave Gambella.

We waited for two days after which we were told that Berhanu had at last been cleared and his identity card had been sent to police headquarters in Goré, the provincial capital. We could collect it any time and proceed to Addis. In Goré the identity card was produced without any fuss and only three days after leaving Gambella we were pushing through celebrating crowds on the outskirts of Addis Ababa. Berhanu was back for *Timkat*. He never expressed much feeling but he seemed pleased.

I had the impression that Berhanu was one of those men who never ever get ruffled, but I was wrong. There was tragic news of him a few months later. He had been involved in a violent quarrel in the city, and in the mistaken belief that he had killed his opponent, Berhanu had shot himself dead.

7

On Foot to the Mago Valley

Our abortive attempts to get to the Mago Valley during the Omo trip led to the conclusion that in practice there is only one way to get there; you fly to Baco, hire pack animals and walk. I forget how many times I have flown to Baco; it has always been a refuelling place during chartered air recces of the south-west. But to travel in a group with camping gear you need a bigger aeroplane, and on our second attempt at the valley we flew on a scheduled flight by C-47 when everyone else, it seemed, was travelling with a fatted goat to visit relatives in Gemu-Gofa.

The passengers normally sit along both sides of the aircraft, facing each other, tube train style, across the gangway. The day we flew they sat only on one side for the canvas seats opposite had all been strapped out of the way to make room for the cargo, a troublesome pile of heterogeneous bundles, beds, boxes, a motor bike (imported by a Peace Corps volunteer) and goats. With sacks tied around their necks like sleeping-bags the goats were stacked and roped along with the other baggage. Mostly they lay quiescent, bleating now and again, heads craning about to see and eyes blinking, but occasionally there would be short bursts of violent struggling. I was suspicious from the start about the old billy-goat in front of me. He seemed to lie quiet only to gather strength. I was correct about it for during the flight he twice broke loose and flopped and kicked up and down the gangway with one hind leg thrust through the bottom of his sack. It drew about as much attention as a hat falling off a rack. The steward simply pulled himself up from his seat at the back and restacked the goat.

I travelled with a game-guard I hadn't worked with before, a big powerful fellow called Alemo, who was reputed to be a stalwart when sober though less co-operative when he was drunk.

They didn't serve drink on the plane but I did note that, like most of the other passengers, Alemo had a liking for sweets. When the steward came to us with his tray, having gone back repeatedly to replenish it, Alemo grabbed a customary handful.

My other companion was Flamingo Feathers who did not appear to enjoy flying. He sat beside me with his slouch hat on his knee, gripping the edge of the seat and staring straight in front as if he were waiting for an injection. Further down the row, next but one to Flamingo, a woman in black, who had my heart-felt sympathy, was making muffled little noises as she vomited into her shawl. Jean was not with us. She had stayed behind in Addis, more than fully occupied with the chores of motherhood. For a while her safari days were over.

Landing at Baco airport with tents and safari boxes does not place one in the strongest bargaining position when it comes to hiring pack animals. With a Land-Rover you can always pretend that you would be just as content to drive on and try elsewhere, but sitting by the airstrip with a heap of safari gear you can't convincingly pretend anything at all. Everyone else does the pretending.

'It's a bad year for donkeys,' they say. 'We need them all in town. It would hardly be worth our while to hire them out, there is so much work for them to do here.' Etc.

It goes on for days while the haggling centres not only on the hire rates, but the compensation price for any animals that might fail to come back, and whether there is a job for a muleteer. Appointments are made and broken and minds and donkeys are changed overnight.

Finally when contracts have been written and signed and enough money has been paid in advance, there is the problem of saddlery and loading-up. On that occasion in Baco I had no saddlery and had to rely on local stuff. That meant old sacks and skins and a long strip of rawhide knotted so as to form a loop in the middle. There is no saddletree of any sort. To pack a donkey or mule you balance the load on the 'saddle', place the loop on top of the load, then pass the free ends of the leather under the animal's belly, up the other side, through the loop and back again, repeating the process several times. It needs two people to do it, one on either side. The load is held in place by the tightness of the straps against the animal's belly and the muleteers usually do the tightening by heaving on the leathers with one knee on the beast's flank. I have seen donkeys stagger off, grunting and breaking wind, drawn up in the middle like a Lancashire black pudding. After a mile or two the load usually shifts and the leathers slacken off. From time to time, depending on the nature of the load and the skill of the packers, the straps have to be retightened.

With a personable young lad as a guide and packer and by walking until dark, we covered, I should say, about ten miles the day we finally got under way. There were many stops and starts. It is important to leave as soon as you are able, even if there are only a couple of hours of daylight left, otherwise by morning someone will have found a new reason for delay. We camped on a knoll after travelling through verdant savanna which differed in no great respect from that which clothes the western edge of the highlands. It was March and although it had rained during the day the night was clear and bright. A bush-baby called plaintively from somewhere above us. The guards laughed as they chattered. They seemed to get on well with each other and with the donkey boy. I turned in after an hour's satisfying contemplation by the fire.

It was shortly after midnight when I was startled out of my sleep by angry shouts and curses. I lay listening for a few minutes. There was a voice I didn't recognise. Perhaps a nocturnal traveller had tripped over someone; the guards had not bothered to put their tents up. Or perhaps they had caught a thief. Then came the familiar and ominous sound of a rifle bolt-action. I rushed out like a rabbit from a ferret-hole. Glaring at each other across the fire, which someone had revived, were my two guards and two policemen. Nearby the lad from Baco was slowly and sullenly rolling up his blanket.

The way I understood it, the boy owed somebody fifty dollars and his creditor had alleged that he was running away. With surprising zeal the police had followed us from Baco and wouldn't even consider my on-the-spot offers of bail. Our guide was marched away into the darkness. Alemo shouldered his rifle and slammed on his hat. He would be back with another guide by sunrise, he said, and he too strode off into the night.

Flamingo and I stared into the fire. I decided that if Alemo was not back by noon we would press on without him. With four donkeys to herd along and slipping loads to cope with, progress would be slow and Alemo, if he did come back, would easily catch up with us. If he didn't, the two of us would have to manage. I was anxious to get far away from Baco as soon as possible or they would probably come after us to arrest the donkeys too.

At sunrise Alemo was back with a wizened little gnome of a man called Anksha. He had offered himself as a guide the day before but I had turned him down in favour of the youth. Terms of hire were soon settled, we had been through it all before and I really did not care all that much whether the man came or not. I inoculated the donkeys against trypanosomiasis and loaded up. Anksha set to with a zest which, though I did not know it at the time, was highly out of character and never to be witnessed again.

We saw no one during the rest of that day; we followed a path through the long *Hyparrhenia* grass which led us westwards between steep-sided hills. There was the same empty quietness about the country which had struck me on the descent from Goré to Gambella, but now it was wet and green. Tsetse flies settled silently, bit voraciously and were off before you could swat them. They came only in ones and twos though, and were not unbearable. Anksha traipsed along in front, trying to establish the idea that he was a guide and intended to have nothing to do with herding donkeys. He carried a gourd as his water bottle, done up in a sort of grass net and slung over his shoulder on a grass rope. He made the rope himself by rolling a few stalks together against his leg. He could produce a serviceable twine in a few seconds.

I felt mildly encouraged when Anksha made a detour off the track to fill his gourd at a hidden water-hole. He had obviously been at least this far before. He disturbed a bushbuck as he scrambled down into the gulley. It bounded into view, stared at us, and leapt back towards Anksha. He never saw it. It was a young male, a light rufus colour. It looked slender and trim by comparison with the near-black, shaggy-haired specimens which live in the high mountains. The difference, though, is only one of race.

We came to the Mago Valley at about midday. It appeared, as valleys often do, suddenly. We stood on its eastern wall, gazing down into a flat-bottomed trough about twenty-five miles long and more than half that distance across. The far side was formed by the long ridge of the Mursé hills. Beyond that and out of sight, stretching westwards to the Omo River, was a great waterless plain, scored with gulleys and scattered with thorn trees, which the Italians had dramatically charted 'The Plain of Death'. The Mago River was invisible somewhere in a broad belt of solid green bush which occupied the middle of the valley floor. On either side, away from the river, the bush thinned out in a patchwork of vegetation which showed up the drainage pattern of the valley.

The plan was to walk down our side of the Mago River, then cross it just above its confluence with the Omo and return along the western side of the valley, recrossing at the northern end. Anksha agreed that it could be done; he knew a way through the thicket to cross the Mago. I asked him where we could camp that night. He pointed south and said, 'Neri.' The Neri is a stream which rises in the Baco highlands and skirts the town on its way to the Mago. The wall of the valley was a succession of thicket-choked gulleys and as far as I could make out the Neri flowed in the third one down from where we were standing. It didn't look all that far away and the nearside of the valley floor appeared to be open enough to be easy going.

We worked our way down to the bottom. The still, hot air was stupefying but for the first hour or two I was too busy and much too excited to care. It was at once obvious that, as game country, Mago was something out of the ordinary in Ethiopia. Every few yards there was something worth stopping for. I urged the others to go ahead with the donkeys to the river and set up camp there.

Herds of hartebeest, identical with those at Murlé, snorted and galloped a zig-zag course through the acacias. Some had tiang running with them. There were Grant's gazelle, lesser kudu, reedbuck, oribi, defassa waterbuck and tracks and signs of elephant, buffalo, zebra and leopard. I followed tracks which showed that giraffe had been about that very morning. Later I saw a score of them cantering in and out of view among the trees, their unbelievable forms rocking in slow motion as neck and hindquarters see-sawed upon the high forelegs. Some had deep, red-brown coats patterned with a network of fine white lines – the reticulate variety. Others were yellowish like the Sudanese race, an interesting range of colour in the same herd.

Nowhere in Ethiopia had I encountered such a variety of big game in so small an area. It was not that there was game in great abundance but it was enough to be able to note the mere presence of such a spectrum of wild animals. In any case, in the full heat of the afternoon, one could not expect to see the valley in a state of tumult. Sensible beasts, like a gerenuk I happened to pick out, would be standing quietly in the shade. He sprinted for another patch of thicket when I got too close. Gone in an instant. Just the pure white patches on each side of his tail bobbing for a moment among the twigs. Further east, gerenuk sport only a pair of narrow, whitish stripes. Another puzzling change of colour schemes.

In a dried-up wallow hole the skeleton of an elephant, complete except for the ivory, lay bleaching in the sun. Its bones had been cleaned by the succession of scavengers which starts with the vultures and ends with the tiny dermestid beetles which thrive upon dried fragments of skin. Baked in the mud beside the bones were the prints of human feet; the only sign of man, as my donkey party had long since disappeared from view.

The afternoon heat-lull hung in the valley as an oppressive stillness. Insects whined and hummed in a background to the lethargic cooing of doves. The occasional alarm call of birds disturbed came as tiny unexpected bursts of energy from the

Termite mound – Jean sets the scale

Somali wild ass in the Danakil Desert

Swayne's hartebeest, adult female and young

Greater kudu, male, near Awash River

Burchell's zebra in the Nachisar Plains

Beisa oryx, Awash

drowsing bush. I swigged the last of the tepid water from my bottle and started off for the camp.

Only after half an hour's hard walking did I realise how utterly sapped I had become: I was quite half-witted with fatigue.

'Salt,' I remember thinking, 'gone on ahead with the water.'

Left, right, left, right; feet had a rhythm of their own, nothing to do with me. They were pounding the earth and mildly throbbing somewhere far below. Plod, plod, plod.

'Thorn bush in the way . . . going to hurt . . . not very big, though, can't possibly break step and turn aside.' Trip, stumble, stinging scratches. Left, right, left.

'Binoculars weigh a ton, arm too heavy to hold them up.'

I'm not sure how long it went on, a couple of hours perhaps, but I had begun to think I would never see water again when I reached the Neri River. It was unbelievable; a tinkling, babbling, silver stream. Flamingo Feathers lay in the shade, knees drawn up and his hat over his face. Alemo, with his back against a log, scrubbed idly at his teeth with a twig. Donkeys nosed among the rushes and someone's socks hung out to dry. I felt tremendously glad to be home.

The Neri was well placed for a camp site and we made it our base for several days. The river itself, like other permanent streams of the Lower Omo system, was well wooded with high *Tamarindus* and acacia trees shading a dense, tangled undergrowth of bushes and shrubs festooned with lianas and interlaced with succulent climbers. Each morning, from the tree-tops, colobus monkeys would rouse us with a throaty gargling chorus before they went to breakfast. White-browed coucals, big cuckoos which build their own nests, bubbled up and down the scale. And of course there were doves. Not just the common interminable cooers but an endearing little anglophile among the emerald-spotted wood doves. It came very close to a rendering of 'Rule Britannia' before abandoning its song to a tumbling diminuendo.

Away from the drainage lines the bush thinned out into open grassland with tall, flat-topped *Acacia tortilis* trees, much loved by giraffe. Lower bushes and shrubs formed discrete clumps of thicket. Common among them were the weeping forms of toothbrush trees (*Salvadora persica*) whose twigs chew up so nicely into brush-ends. It was first-rate cover for the smaller antelopes. Oribi and reedbuck abounded: the 'small brown buck' of the pothunters. Towards the centre of the valley, on either side of the Mago River, the bush thickened to an impenetrable belt of thicket four or five miles wide. Impenetrable, that is, to a few struggling men and donkeys but riddled with the tracks and trails of buffalo and elephant.

It is a familiar fact that wildlife tends to be richer in variety where two different habitats adjoin. You can see more kinds of birds, for instance, at the edge of a woodland than within the woods or out in the open meadow. Hedgerows demonstrate this ecological edge effect beautifully, if somewhat artificially, as long strips of woodland between fields. In the Mago Valley the distribution of surface and soil water and the mosaic of vegetation had produced a sort of disseminate edge effect in addition to the habitat diversity. The result was that throughout the valley one could find animals of the open plains such as Grant's gazelle, oryx and zebras (Burchell's and Grevy's) within a stone's throw of cover-loving animals such as buffalo, bushbuck and waterbuck. In all we saw or found positive evidence of nearly thirty species of mammals from the size of a dikdik upwards.

The possibilities for developing and protecting the valley were very exciting for there was reason to believe that the game was largely resident there throughout the year. It did not need much imagination to see a system of carefully laid-out motor tracks leading with studied informality to viewing platforms at selected vantage points. One might see buffalo wallowing and blowing, plastered with mud. Or perhaps a pride of lions at a kill. Antelope visiting a salt lick or a water-hole in the cool of the morning; timid yet often majestic, listening, pausing, testing the air, lingering a few moments then passing quietly out of view. There is no better way to watch wild animals than to watch them without being detected.

It would all need careful planning. Setting up the area for

visitors would itself have an unavoidable impact on the valley. For those who value such things (and the solitude-seekers are always the first to lose out) the feeling of remoteness could disappear for a start. But good management can do a lot. Parks do need to be managed, with or without visitors. The very act of declaring a park sets the land apart from surroundings which get different treatment. A park becomes an 'ecological island' and as such it is really an artificial entity. The movements of animals and other natural events are influenced by the fact that they are being allowed inside a specially protected area. Man creates parks and wildlife sanctuaries for his own purposes and it is important, when it comes to managing them, to have the purposes well defined. If the objectives of a park have not been decided, people will never agree on how best to run it, and although management by burning grass or planting trees may not arouse much passion, the emotionally-charged controversy which rages over issues such as whether or not to cull an elephant population can be quite alarming.

In the Mago Valley, for some years' time, a policy of total protection could safely be adopted. Less than a mile from our camp on the Neri River the remains of three buffalos lay rotting in the grass. Above them, hanging in the trees out of reach of hyaenas, the hides were stretched to dry on a framework of branches. The hides were not worth much and the poachers had left them there until they were ready to be collected. A little further away, a jackal lay dying in a steel trap. It was dead when we found it next morning. The gin-trap, an imported type openly on sale in Addis Ababa's modern hardware shops, had undoubtedly been intended for a leopard. The trappers were probably trading leopard skins for bullets or rifles supplied by a middle-man who would sell the skins to a bigger dealer in the capital. They would eventually be smuggled out of the country. More likely than not, in a cargo of legitimate skins, hides and skins being Ethiopia's second biggest export commodity. Despite legislation, the leopard-skin trade continues to flourish.

I asked Anksha who the poachers were. I had never heard of

the tribe but according to Anksha they came down to the valley floor from the east solely to hunt game. From the other side of the valley, the Mursé, a cattle-owning tribe, did much the same while their cattle were grazed on the Mursé hills and westwards on to the Plain of Death. Tsetse flies kept the valley itself free from cattle.

There are twenty-two species of tsetse fly (*Glossina*) ranging over more than four million square miles of Africa. They are all bloodsuckers, able rapidly to gorge twice their weight at a sitting if you don't feel them in time. By carrying infective protozoans (*Trypanosoma*) in their saliva, tsetse flies transmit trypanosomiasis, which in man takes the form of sleeping sickness and in cattle is a disease, often fatal, called nagana. Other domestic animals are affected too. A few species of tsetse (*Glossina morsitans* and its allies), having a much greater range than the others and inhabiting wooded grasslands, are much more important to man and stock than the rest. It is not that men and stock are particularly sought after by tsetse – wild pigs generally seem to be the favourite host – but a variety of animals are made use of and man and his animals get included. One species of fly, at least, will even tackle crocodiles' gums! Tsetse breed slowly compared with, say, houseflies which are similar-sized insects. Once inseminated by a male the female tsetse produces one larva every ten days for the rest of her life, but she only lives for about fifteen weeks. She deposits the larva in a shady spot and it at once burrows into the soil and becomes a pupa, looking rather like the pupa of a housefly. About a month later it bursts out as an adult tsetse.

It is difficult not to have mixed feelings about tsetse flies. At best, they are infuriating insects which employ unsporting tactics such as alighting beneath a camp chair and assailing one's buttocks through the fabric. At worst, and in sober analysis, they could be described as a scourge of man and stock. And yet were it not for the tsetse, some of the finest National Parks in East Africa would never have been created and could instead have become miserable tracts of eroded cattle land. In many parts of Africa 'fly country' has remained ecologically healthy while adjacent fly-free regions, which happen not to suit the flies, have been reduced to sub-desert by overgrazing and general misuse. There are those who regard the tsetse with affection.

There were fish in the Neri River and before moving off I caught a few tiddlers in a sack for identification. At that moment a lean, sharp-featured old man appeared in a scarecrow hat; the first stranger we had seen for four days. He ran a beady but professional eye over my catch and looked at me with genuine pity. From a pack on his back he unwrapped a bundle of dried fish strips and gave me some. In Amharic he advised me to go further upstream. There were deep pools there, he said, where all the big ones were. A nice old chap, I thought, but the others said he was a bit crazy. I cooked his fish strips and ate them with onions, Enterovioform tablets and no ill-effects.

We pursued a complicated course down the valley and it soon became clear that Anksha had no more idea than the rest of us where we could cross the Mago. We tried cutting the thicket-belt at what appeared to be a narrow point but it would have taken days and we could not carry enough water for days. We followed buffalo trails but they never led to anything except a state of utter exhaustion and a feeling of having been flagellated with thorns. Most of the time the donkeys were either entangled with their loads in the thicket or lost in another branch of the maze. There was an underlying anxiety, too, about what we might come face to face with. At one point, in a gap near the edge of the thicket, we halted abruptly, while a herd of about twenty buffalo thundered past at a lumbering charge. More correctly they were retreating from someone or something in the thicket which alarmed them more than we did. Anyway, we did not find a way through and were obliged to stay on the east side of the Mago for the whole length of the valley. We eventually came out on the bank of the Omo River.

Thicket and forest now merged and lay as a solid woven carpet of vegetation from the river to the eastern hills where it stretched in tatters between the spurs. This was the other side of the barrier which had blocked our journey north from Murlé.

There was a clearing in the riverside forest; trampled vegetation, broken gourds and corn stalks in soil tilled with simple hoes. All the signs that a settlement was not far away.

'Karo' was what Anksha called the tribe, 'Mago Karo' when he wanted to be more precise. There were a few youths where we camped, a bit further on, wading about in a swamp, spearing catfish. Later they brought their chief. He was a long, stringy man who spoke in a high-pitched gabble and he and his friends didn't look or sound at all pleased to see us. But they soon softened up and we had no trouble. The following morning the chief led us through the forest to the mouth of the Mago River. It trickled as a small stream out of the forest and into the muddy water of the Omo. It was sufficient, all the same, to keep some very large pools filled throughout the dry season and to prevent our walking up the river bed.

The only point at which one could cross to the other side was where the Mago entered the Omo and it proved to be out of the question with donkeys. It involved edging along stretches of vertical bank and holding on to a tree where footholds failed. It was not that the Mago River could not be crossed. There was a relatively easy ford at the northern end, but the idea of a round trip had to be abandoned. With our resources, there was no way of recrossing in the south.

There was not, in fact, very much difference between the two sides of the valley. I flew up and down it later on, both by fixed-wing aircraft and by helicopter. There is no doubt that by flying you see much more, and more comfortably, than you do on foot. For censusing the conspicuous animals it is the obvious method to use. But you miss a lot from an aircraft: the tracks and sounds of secretive or nocturnal things, the birdlife, the plants. There is no chance to examine anything from the air, to stop and listen. Perception is by sight alone and the experience is correspondingly restricted, like watching a film instead of taking part in it as one of the cast.

On that first safari into Mago it was probably just as well that we did not attempt too much. On the return journey Anksha virtually gave up. He lay in his tent each morning intoning his impressions of dying-noises. Alemo had to evict him forcibly. His complaint, if he had any physical complaint, defied diagnosis and I gave him all the pills I had which could be guaranteed not to make him any worse. I was not a hundred per cent fit myself and a number of the bites and scratches which I had accumulated had turned septic and were developing into tropical sores. There was a dispiriting stiffening of the armpits and groin as I trudged back up the valley. But I was glad to know that I would be returning to Mago.

There was a day to wait for the plane when we got to Baco and that night I visited the bar where I felt certain I would find the old mechanic who had done the axle job on the Land-Rover. He was a likeable chap and it was worth buying him a drink just to see his beaming, toothless grin. He wasn't there. When I made enquiries they told me he had been killed the year before, in a truck which had rolled off that road through the mountains.

Some constables arrived before the plane. Nothing personal, just a baggage check to foil hijackers. They had the time of their lives with the safari boxes. Three of them devoted half an hour to the job. I managed to maintain a fixed rictus while they tore open packets of sterile dressings from the first aid box and probed about in my coffee jar for hidden bombs. I confess to a secret feeling of cynical amusement as I boarded the plane. The rucksack on my back was the one piece of baggage to which I would have easy access during the flight. They didn't ask to see it.

8

Ups and Downs in the North

The longest single period I ever spent in the northern highlands was a fortnight during which I was involved in a boundary survey of the Simien Mountains National Park. There was never any other reason for spending much time there. As the Abyssinia of old, the highlands of the north have been subjected to a longer period of occupation by peasant farmers than has anywhere else in Ethiopia. As a result there isn't much left of the natural scene.

But the Simien Mountains are exceptional and it had been deemed worth the struggle to try to establish a park there. I shall not go into details of the struggling which had already gone on, for the story, vividly told, has itself filled a book.* It should be pointed out though that in Ethiopia, and especially among the northern highlanders, land is jealously coveted and cultivable patches of it have probably aroused more murderous passions in men than has anything else in that part of the world. Yet more often than not those who till the soil are not the owners. They are sharecroppers who have to give up half or more of their produce in tithe to their landlords. When a plot is owner-cultivated it is frequently on a communal basis in which every new claimant, when he comes of age, has an inalienable right to a share of it. This necessitates periodic redivision of the land into ever-decreasing portions so that the owners finish up with fragmented plots which are hardly worth owning. The laws of land tenure, however, are to an outsider mysterious and bewildering in their complexity and one of the few generalisations which can be made is that any attempt to interfere with the system on a large scale can be relied upon to cause trouble, at personal, community and political levels.

* *From the Roof of Africa* by Clive Nicol, published by Hodder & Stoughton, Ltd, London, 1972.

Because of these problems it was only after several years of hard work by a number of dedicated individuals that in October 1969 a small part of the Simien Mountains became a gazetted National Park by imperial proclamation in the *Negarit Gazeta*, the official journal in which all legal announcements are published. Not that this meant very much to the people actually living in the Simien Mountains but it was an official step in the right direction and was well worth following up. In June of the following year an expedition of officials and others thought to be concerned with the park was sent to Simien to explain and point out the boundaries to the local inhabitants. My part in the affair was merely to translate the carefully-worded boundary description into something meaningful on the ground: to interpret the legal jargon, which was printed in English as well as Amharic, and to show what it meant in terms of distances and directions in the Simien Mountains. Those who had originally done the boundary work had long since left the country.

We flew to Gondar, the capital of Begemder, in which province the park lay. The idea was to collect a senior police official from the provincial police headquarters and drive with him straightaway to Simien. The major, however, was not quite ready to leave. On the day that he was ready we received word that the Governor of the Simien *Awraja* had publicly declared his intention to be totally unco-operative with us when we got there. This piece of intelligence caused the Provincial Vice-Governor in Gondar to write a letter to the Simien man. I never knew whether it demanded his co-operation, requested it or simply wished him well, but it took another three days.

I killed some of this time by looking at Gondar's ruins, especially those within the old royal compound where past kings had made their homes. King Fasil (1632–1667) started it, using the skill of Portuguese architects and masons. The 17-acre compound lies within a basalt wall with a dozen gates, each built for different ceremonial occasions or for the passage of specified classes of people such as the various nobles, court musicians, judges and so on. There was a church service in progress that morning and the beggars were gathering outside the appropriate gate. Fasil's castle itself still dominates the compound. It is a big, two-storey construction built from rough-hewn basalt stones with a battlement parapet surrounding a flat roof. There are four domed towers and a taller, square tower with steps leading up. From the top I looked out over the other, lesser buildings of the compound.

In equally cheerless accommodation, and behind bars, there were lions and a leopard. I went to see them. The leopard had developed what is technically known as a stereotyped behaviour pattern. In more anthropomorphic terms it paced the tiny floor-space of its cage with a terrible fretfulness, an intensity of anxiety which one felt and hoped must soon subside. Surely it could not keep it up. At each turn at the end of the cage it knocked its head against the bars. Its nose was raw and bleeding. It had been in the cage, they said, for seven years.

I found it a relief to turn to the lions. They lay dozing among the bones of their last meal, twitching at the flies and now and again looking up to appraise the audience. Lions do well in captivity, accepting confinement with a yawn and a sigh of resignation. And if breeding success is any measure of contentment in captive animals then they must find the life to their liking for they produce cubs in embarrassing numbers for those who have to feed or find homes for them. At the castle they tried to give me two.

You may suspect that I was not properly impressed by Gondar's castle compound. It is not, by any standards, outstanding among Ethiopia's historic attractions. It does not compare in antiquity with, say, the stele of Axum. These granite monoliths, up to seventy feet high, are presumed to have been erected seventeen centuries ago to mark the tombs of pagan royalty. Nor does Gondar possess anything to match the stone churches of Lalibella in Wollo province. But then I am no historian and even before these great monuments I am apt to be more strongly affected by the state of the living than by the glory of the past, so I had better return to my story.

When the day came for us to leave we got away from Gondar just before lunchtime. This came as a last-minute reprieve from yet another meal of roast veal and cabbage followed by crème caramel. They were very proud of this dish at the hotel but they had no alternative to offer guests who got marooned there. I had been having trouble with the music in Gondar too. They played it every day through loudspeakers set around the central square and the loudspeakers did not synchronise. I find it impossible to ignore music which I can't switch off, even when it's music I don't like. I suppose there was probably some place in that square where, had I stood stock-still with my head at the correct angle, the speakers would have been synchronised, but I never found the spot.

The Governor of Simien *Awraja* lived in Devarik, a village on the main road about sixty miles north of Gondar and the starting point of the mule trek into the Simien Mountains. We arrived, in a complaining Land-Rover, in the early afternoon and at once sought out the Governor. He was a big, middle-aged man with a thick frizz of white hair. He spoke in a powerful voice as he emerged from his house and thrust a hand from his *shamma* to greet us. Ethiopians are great meeters and greeters but in the course of the conversation which followed the salaams I realised that this man actually enjoyed being obstructive and obstinate. He looked upon it as a game, a battle of wits, like chess. He offered hospitality so that we could play the game in comfort. We sat late into the night, among the shadows of his lamplit house, drinking *talla* and *tej* – and arguing. It was all very good-natured for it was obviously a favourite pastime. The position was simple: the Governor's presence was essential if our trip was to be a success but the Governor didn't want to be involved.

Eventually a compromise was reached and the Governor agreed to send his secretary with us as his personal representative. During the second day the debate centred on practical problems of the secretary's payment and *per diem* allowance and the expected duration of the trip. Throughout long periods of the discussion the Governor wore a look of intense, almost pained concentration: he was gouging his auditory passage with a silver ear-pick, a thing like a miniature spoon with an ornate handle.

When a settlement appeared to have been reached negotiations for horses and mules began. This deal went much faster and the desire for haste on the part of the owners was understandable: several of the animals were about to die. The best were merely emaciated and dreadfully galled. Ethiopian highlanders are often enviably good riders but their neglect of both pack and riding animals is appalling. It is hard to understand, for instance, why a narrow thong of hard rawhide should be used to hobble a mule or donkey when a softer, broader band would do the job without lacerating its flesh. It is not just lack of sympathy. The efficiency of the injured beast is reduced and the fact is recognised and lamented by those who cause the injuries. Still, I was glad that the mule negotiations hadn't taken long, for the previous night in Devarik had been a singularly unedifying experience. The rooms we had been forced to occupy, though managed by well-meaning people, were dank little closets and the toilet arrangements were most unsatisfactory. You crouched in the corner of the yard behind a large sheet of tin which rested on your head. My unexpected request for washing water had brought me a cupful in an old tin can. I was very anxious to be off and sleep in the palatial comfort of my tiny tent.

When we finally straggled up the hill out of Devarik our party was nearly thirty strong. The police major had mustered a squad of half a dozen constables, there was a young man from the Mapping Institute, two fellows from the Wildlife Department, mule boys and general hangers on. The most interesting character was a tall man in a red woolly cap who bore the title of *Kegnazmatch*. The title itself (Marshal of the Right) is nothing remarkable. Such titles of military origin came to be bestowed as civil honours and are quite commonplace. The Governor in Devarik was the equivalent of a Count and his secretary who accompanied us was a *Balambaras* – Commander of the Fort.

The intriguing thing about this *Kegnazmatch* was the respect he commanded among the populace of the district. He elicited, I noticed, a fawning response from nearly everyone we passed. He was obviously a most important member of our team. I later discovered that he was the leader of the local *nach lebash*. This

At Lake Abiata: Fish eagle

Black-headed weaver and nest

Yellow-billed stork

Soemmering's gazelle near Awash River

Beira antelope, Marmar Mountains

literally means white uniform but is best translated as plain clothes. In remote highland areas the *nach lebash* serve as police deputies and informers. Their salary is nominal but the opportunities for augmenting it can be imagined.

For several hours we climbed gradually eastwards on to the Simien massif, a vast tilted block of land sloping gently southwards from a vertical north face. The park was on the north-western part of the massif so as to include a section of the high plateau and a stretch of the northern precipice nearly twenty miles long. It amounted to about sixty square miles in all.

The lower levels of the massif are now cultivated and elsewhere most of the tree cover has been destroyed. Only remnants of the natural vegetation show that at one time the lower levels must have been clothed by a beautiful woodland of *Hagenia* and juniper trees with St John's wort and giant heath higher up. *Hagenia* is a pleasing tree with a nice rounded form and fine autumn colours. It grows on mountains throughout Africa but in Ethiopia it has special significance: the fruits are the source of the highland man's anti-tapeworm dose. It is consumed as a regular monthly purgative which has been found necessary because of the prevailing lack of sanitation and the Ethiopian predilection for raw beef. Uncooked meat is a conspicuous feature of high-class tables and important feasts. At the few of the latter which I have attended it has been carried to the guests as half a cow suspended from a pole across the shoulders of two bearers. You have a little sharp knife with which to carve off the section of your choice and for piquancy you dip chunks of it into an equally raw preparation of red peppers.

The part of the plateau within the park lies at around 11,000 feet. It was cool and fresh when we got there, with a breeze blowing across the open grassland. We walked along the edge of a valley towards Sankaber where a cosy *tukul* type of house had once been the home of Clive Nicol, a previous game warden.

In the shelter of the valley scores of gelada baboons came into view, hunched forms dotting the rough green pasture on the lee side; each was meticulously selecting its diet from the grasses and herbs. The males had manes of long hair which fell about their shoulders as a mantle, pale against the thick, dark brown coat. Geladas are found only in the mountains of Ethiopia to the north of Addis Ababa. In Simien they spend their nights on the cliff face, coming up to feed during the day. They have patches of naked red skin on their chests which the books will tell you have given rise to the name 'bleeding heart baboons'. Everyone I know calls them geladas. Facially they look like monkeys for they have relatively short, rounded muzzles instead of the dog-like snouts of other baboons.

The troop we saw was really a temporary association of several separate family groups, each composed of a male with a harem and youngsters. It had been found that the young bachelors form groups too, though none of this was apparent as we looked down on the scattered herd. A whole complex and delicately balanced social organisation was being maintained with nothing more obvious than a few grunts and gestures. Yet recent research by British scientists has brought to light a gelada vocabulary of nearly 30 distinct noises, many of which are used to keep members of the family or group in touch with each other when they have become dispersed: apparently they learn to recognise each other's voices.

The Simien park can actually boast three mammals which are not found outside Ethiopia. The Simien fox, which is not unlike a big European fox in general appearance, occurs only in Simien and the mountains of Arussi and Bale. But the walia ibex is *the* animal which must always be thought of in connection with Simien for this wild goat is found nowhere else. The walia is a big ibex; an adult male can weigh up to 270 pounds and his massive ringed horns may well be over a yard long. In 1963 the total population of walia was estimated by Leslie Brown to be about 150 to 200. A serious decline had obviously taken place since H. C. Maydon wrote about walia in 1925. He could see then more walia in a single day than Dr Brown was able to find in a week.

The status of walia became a matter for international concern.

They were worried about, written about, photographed, filmed, televised and, in Ethiopia, adopted as the emblem of wildlife conservation. But they still remained uncomfortably close to extinction. At the time of writing the walia appear to be holding their own, or perhaps increasing, but as I was to see for myself in Simien, they continue to lead a precarious existence in more ways than one.

At Sankaber the first mule died and thereafter we began to replace the worst of the mules with donkeys hired from Simien villagers; some of the replacements were themselves replaced before the end of the trip and the final settling-up must have been a complicated transaction. I was glad that on that occasion it was not my business.

After a night at Sankaber we trekked eastwards along the edge of the escarpment, skirting a breathtaking abyss with a sheer drop of some 2,000 feet or more to reach the village of Geech which lay at about 12,000 feet above sea-level. As a boundary commission it was necessary for us to stop at each village and hamlet to carry out the public relations work and in Ethiopian eyes there is no doubt that we must have appeared as a very official and important delegation. We had the right status symbols: revolvers in shoulder holsters, fairly modern rifles with ammunition to match and even a sub-machine gun. I forgot who brought this last piece of equipment; I don't believe that he ever carried it, and happily he never had cause to use it. It was always to be seen on the shoulder of a proud gun-bearer, a grizzled little man, rather too little to be able to wear the crossed bandoliers as carelessly as he would have liked.

Ethiopians carry firearms the way Englishmen carry fountain pens (or should it be ball-points now?) but often, as among the Simien villagers, they are ancient weapons and there is no proper ammunition for them. This does not seem to bother anybody. Once, further north, I remarked about it to a very tough-looking Tigrean. His rifle was an eight-millimetre Mannlicher while his belt was stuffed with ·303 ammunition. Not only was this the wrong calibre but the brass cartridges were an entirely different size and shape and wouldn't even fit into the rifle. The old poacher laughed at me, patiently, as if I were a child who hadn't yet learned how to load a gun. He showed me by vigorously battering a round of ·303 between two stones until it could be rammed into the breech. 'Now it is good,' he said.

It was in the Simien that the Oligocene lavas which capped the Ethiopian Plateau reached their greatest thickness. One theory is that the Simien lavas were extruded from a gigantic Hawaiian-type volcano whose crater was at the north-eastern edge of the existing mountain block. The present south-sloping massif is presumed to be part of the original gently-sloping cone of the volcano. Parts of the precipitous north face show in profile the alternating layers of harder and softer lavas selectively weathered so as to appear as jutting and receding strips. I say this is shown in parts for the Simien Mountains have been fashioned into the most fantastic mountain scenery to be found anywhere in Africa. Torrents and waterfalls have dissected the cliff face into an irregular series of deep gorges and chasms. Sections of the plateau have been cut off as outliers and these have been further weathered into spectacular crags and pinnacles by the action of rain, wind and widely fluctuating temperatures on the hard volcanic rock. It is wild and violent scenery but the forces which produced it are still slowly and imperceptibly at work.

We were lucky to have good visibility for it was the end of June and the big rains were imminent, but it stayed dry most of the time and there were fine clear views every day. It was a little frustrating to be on the boundary team. I had no time to myself, no chance to wander off and spy for walia or watch the birds. There is no unique spectacle of birds in Simien, nothing which cannot be seen elsewhere in the Ethiopian highlands, but the setting makes a difference. White-collared pigeons hurtle into the void with a brief passing hiss of speed. Choughs wheel and yelp as they do off the Cornish cliffs, and in Simien, a lammergeyer might pass within a few yards, riding the air currents on long gliding-wings like a highland albatross.

Watching a lammergeyer, it seems best to overlook the fact that his nearest relatives are vultures. He does not keep company with them himself, and after all, you would never guess his affinities from his appearance. Below he is rust-coloured; above blackish. The head is white with black round the eye and a curious beard of bristles protrudes on either side of the bill: the bearded vulture. He is the perfect glider, a specialist, totally committed to a life of mountains, thermals and open space. With a wingspan of nine feet he is precluded from ever hopping nimbly about the trees. He is the end product of millions of years of selection for the best combination of aerodynamic properties for gliding. Natural selection is an inexorable process, given time for everything to be weighed in the balance. Nature's best design, all things considered, is that which leaves the most offspring to perpetuate it. And it need only be ever so slightly more offspring for the design to become the standard type by displacing the rest, but it does take time. Nowadays such processes can be quantified in a few hours by running the idea through computers.

The bone-smashing habits of lammergeyer are well-known. When the vultures and jackals have scattered the remains of a carcass the lammergeyer will pick up the bones. Bones too big to eat are carried off and deliberately dropped from perhaps 200 feet to be smashed on the rocks below. The same bone-smashing rocks or ossuaries are used habitually. There were at least two at Geech.

We left Geech next day and continued to the eastern end of the park towards Ras Dashan which rose beyond the boundary and at 15,000 feet is Ethiopia's highest peak. Although Ethiopia has the biggest mountain mass in Africa there are much higher mountains in three other African countries. The going was easy as we trod the tussocks cropped close by the cattle and goats of Geech. A group of villagers watched us go by. They stood bare-foot with their white *shammas* pulled across their faces, swathed like corpses against the cold. There was no comfort in the scene that morning; just the bleak moors of the high plateau rolling away from the edge of the earth. In a long procession we walked to our next point accompanied by the rhythmic clatter of the boxes on the pack mules.

Now and again a small brown rat would appear on the surface

only to scuttle along for a few inches and pop into another of the myriad burrows which riddled the turf like a Gruyère cheese. The rats too must have made their mark on the grassland and it occurred to me that they could make up a fair proportion of the staple diet of the Simien foxes. I had watched the foxes stalking and pouncing on small rats in Bale. Yet in Simien the Simien foxes have become unaccountably scarce and to me they are the most interesting and attractive of all Ethiopia's endemic mammals. Again the zoological position is not clear but they are probably most nearly akin to jackals. Their jaws are long and lightly built for snapping up small rodents and birds. They call with a loud screaming yelp, like a vixen's cry but uttered in broad daylight as they move at a fast trot over the moors. The general impression is of a handsome red fox the size of an Alsatian dog. Its coat and brush are thick, luxuriantly and understandably so, for the nights are cold the year round on the high moors and during the day the sun's radiation is intense. With a little breeze you may never feel too hot but you get blistered and frozen by turns. To one accustomed to temperate zones it is as though the whole yearly range of temperatures has been compressed into twenty-four hours, only more so, since the daily range is greater than the annual one on high African mountains. This limits things and puts special demands on others. As a creature faced with winter you can hibernate if you can't carry on, but when winter comes round every night this solution won't do. And for winter-loving forms of life there is the daily sun-ray treatment to contend with. Animals of the mountain tops have to be tolerant of extremes or else they must be able to dodge at times, as the rats do, by going underground. Birds of course can migrate daily up and down the cliff face, thousands of feet in altitude; and for their purposes, equivalent to several degrees of latitude. The choughs roost somewhere down the cliff face but feed on the top.

Plants too may take evasive action and some spend the night in closed sleep. Others like the *Helichrysum* and *Alchemilla* have a silvery down which perhaps protects from frost as well as shielding from the sun. Grasses tend to be tussock-forming so as to give shelter at least to the inner growing shoots. They are often wiry grasses like those of the European moors. They grow with the cushions of everlasting flowers, lady's mantle and sedges where spikes of giant lobelia rise ten or twenty feet above the ground: a truly Afro-alpine mixture.

From the eastern end of the park we began a tortuous descent from the plateau to the lowlands in order to follow the northern boundary westwards back to starting point. The muleteers had a difficult time of it here for the track frequently ran through rocky passes too narrow for the loaded animals. There was a good deal of shouting and struggling and not all the loads came through undamaged. From the foot of the escarpment the plight of the walia was all too apparent. A steep slope was still smouldering from a fire which had been deliberately started by cultivators. The intention had been to burn off a rather gentler bit at the bottom which might for a few years be cultivable. But the flames had travelled upwards and another large patch of mountainside had been denuded of trees and bushes. The summer rains would do the rest and the soil would soon be washed off the parent rock. It would take a long time to come back.

Soil formation is an exceedingly slow process. When the weathering of rock has produced the parent material of rock particles, early colonising plants and simple organisms impart life and an organic component. By the processes of growth and decay the soil is then modified and organically enriched until it will support more demanding plants. These in turn may cause such changes in the soil as to pave the way for other plants. So in the mountains the succession proceeded to the ultimate vegetation formation that each climatic zone would allow; from the lower flowering forests to the highest windswept moorlands. Man is destroying what he can never see replaced, for he lives on a different time-scale.

We saw four walia briefly. They were moving along a ledge high above us, dark brown figures out of earshot and much too far away for a photograph. It is not in the nature of ibex to stray far from the crags and the cliffs but they were obviously no longer able to occupy much potentially favourable habitat. As Leslie Brown had discovered more than a decade before, the walia had become restricted to the most impregnable parts of their former range. Elsewhere they had been shot out or displaced by human activity. Domestic goats now scamper where ibex used to live.

There were many stops on the lowland leg of the journey. We seemed to be falling upon one hamlet after another like a raiding party. Fodder would appear for the animals and popcorn, *injera*, coffee and *talla* for the raiders, often from the tiniest and poorest of dwellings. I never saw a coin change hands and I got the impression that it was all a sort of obligatory hospitality but it was readily given. It was warmer during the lowland stops and we could sit about comfortably. One of the muleteers occupied himself at such times by manufacturing a fly whisk from the tails of his charges. He did it, in a neat zig-zag pattern, on a length of wire looped around his big toe. In Gondar the numerous Orthodox priests invariably carried one of these fly whisks. The boy said he intended to sell his.

The major on these occasions was something of a comedy act. He would flop down, scattering his hat, umbrella and boots about him, and begin to yell for things. Once it was for his feet to be washed. It was obvious that he shouted so many instructions at once that no one could possibly do his bidding and people usually ended up creased with laughter. This didn't upset him; he was a rotund, comic little figure and I never saw him in an ill humour.

Early one afternoon things developed into little short of a circus. We had just pitched camp near one of the hamlets (there was a noticeable shortening of the working day towards the end of the trip) when a rampant donkey chased an unwilling mate into the arena of tents. Had we known there was to be a circus performance we could have arranged the tents in a bigger circle but as the frantic pair pounded around on their restricted circuit pandemonium broke out. Everyone scrambled to snatch possessions out of their path. Cooking pots were trampled, guy ropes

The Simien Mountains

Simien fox, Bale Mountains

Nomad family on the move, Ogaden (boys in foreground from a nearby village)

The man from the salt carava

snapped and tents lurched. Shouting and waving was futile. People started hurling stones at the stallion but they might as well have patted his head for all the notice he took. The mare was constantly catching him squarely in the throat with both rear hooves and even that apparently failed to register. The ardour of a male donkey is a truly wondrous thing.

The problem was ultimately solved when several members of the party rather unsportingly flung themselves upon the mare and held her by the ears. The stallion's response to this was to stop dead in his tracks and look about him for the first time at the havoc he had caused. When he hung his head and looked bashful I could scarcely believe it and the man from the Mapping Institute literally fell down laughing. For the record I should mention that the donkey's sudden shyness was soon overcome.

The lowland settlements were, for the most part, outside the park boundary but the activities of the people were encroaching further and further within the park as they extended up the foot-slopes of the escarpment, burning, cutting fuel, cultivating and grazing their goats on every accessible ledge and terrace. Resettlement of the several hundred people living within the park and strict enforcement of the boundaries would, it was plain, require not only money but strong determined action on the part of the Ethiopian authorities if the Simien park was to become a reality and not just a map.

In bright, warm sunshine we tramped through meadows green and fresh with recent rain. We crossed broad terraces cut by innumerable little streams. We followed rivers and peered down into deep gorges where hamadryas baboons barked their defiance. We stared up at prominent peaks or *ambas* which had names like *Serek amba*, *Angwe amba* and *Chinni amba*. They formed natural boundary beacons below the great precipice.

On our right, falling away to the north, there were lower peaks, crags and jagged ridges and the ever-cultivated terraces dropped sometimes gently into valleys, sometimes in a succession of cliffs, down to the great encircling gorge of the Taccaze; the flowing moat around the fairy-tale land of craggy castles. On the last day I was still in good form for walking and I strode out well ahead of the leading mules. The air was sweet and the water was pure, yet for some perverse, masochistic reason I kept thinking of the sordid little hovel in Devarik where I would have to spend the night. I dimly recalled a hymn; something about a land where 'every prospect pleases . . .' I was in a queer mood that last day.

9

Salt and Brimstone: The Danakil Depression

With some people it's mountains, with others the sea, but that first drive from Assab to Addis kindled in me a certain fascination for deserts. Yet it was more than four years before I could justify anything more than brief visits to relatively accessible parts of the Danakil. Admittedly I had an enviable degree of freedom in planning each year's fieldwork programme but there was an order of priority based on what was already known or suspected about the status of wildlife and the possibilities and need for conservation measures in each province.

The main cause for concern in the Danakil was the status of the Somali wild ass, but a visiting researcher had already carried out a detailed study on the asses as a result of which it had been possible to formulate sound conservation measures for its protection in central Danakil. In addition, the Awash National Park (more about this in chapter 10) had already been created from an old royal hunting preserve and this offered some protection to most of the animals typical of the Danakil. So an ecological reconnaissance survey of the region was fairly low on the list of priorities. It would have to be done eventually, of course, in order to provide the basic data necessary for the nation-wide conservation scheme, but there appeared to be no special urgency about it.

The Ras Mengasha Seyoum thought otherwise. The active and influential prince and Governor of Tigre province considered that Tigre had a lot to offer. Already tourists were flying in to the Danakil Depression to see where sulphur spread its colours over the salty crust of the ancient sea bed. They were flying over volcanoes where molten lava glowed in streaks of liquid red.

And the Ras believed they might be shown big game as an additional attraction. Certainly there were wild asses in the Tigre part of Danakil as well as in Harrar where the wild ass reserve had been proposed. Indeed the Tigre tribesmen spoke of all kinds of wild animals in the Tigre deserts. It was about time that the biologist from the Wildlife Department came and had a look at the area. The biologist went, immediately.

I was lucky to have Hussein Borrissa to go with me. Hussein was a game-guard much in demand by visiting sport-hunters who in turn passed on his name to fellow sportsmen. It was a rule that visiting sport-hunters had to be accompanied on safari by a game-guard and it could make all the difference to a safari if the guard was also a field assistant and not just an imposition. So people asked for Hussein. He was a useful chap to have around; a good skinner, willing to tackle most other jobs in camp and invariably cheerful. The only thing that got him down was the weather in the mountains.

'Very cold me no good,' he told me. 'Hot place me very good.'

'Splendid,' I said, 'we going very hot place.'

On business which need not concern us here I had to call at the Governor's office in Debre Marcos on the way north. The office was on one side of an open square with a flagpole in the middle and the police station and courthouse along the other sides. About twenty highlanders sat in a silent group on the ground with knees drawn up and *shammas* wrapped round against the biting cold, a couple of dozen quiet, grey cones with woolly tops. I didn't pay much attention; there were always such people hanging about courts and offices. Hussein displayed his teeth and most of his gums in one of his regular, expansive grins.

'Teefs,' he said.

'What?'

'Teefs,' he said again, and pointed to the squatters with his chin while he put both wrists together in a handcuffed position.

'Oh, thieves.'

Sure enough, a little later, at 6 p.m., the flag was lowered and everyone had to stand to attention. The squatters rose and as they did so leg irons fell about their ankles. When the ceremony was over they clanked under armed guard down the hill, back to prison until the next day when they would wait again for their cases to be heard.

We took two days getting to Makelle, the capital of Tigre, timing our arrival for office hours only to find that the Ras had gone to Addis Ababa. His secretary was expecting us however and the same day he drafted a letter of introduction, a *dabdab*, to the police at Dallol, an outpost in the Danakil Depression. No other authorities were involved beyond Makelle, which was a relief, for the *dabdab* system wastes hours of precious safari time but is unavoidable if police posts have to be passed or the co-operation of district governors is needed. An open letter from the highest provincial authority 'to whom it may concern' is simply not acceptable. Each district governor expects to receive a sealed letter addressed personally to him and he in turn feels obliged to seal and address a letter to each subordinate authority in his district. Form and the hierarchy must be observed.

While we waited for our letter Hussein made enquiries as to where I could procure a length of steel pipe for I discovered I'd forgotten to bring the lever for the winch. We toured the town inspecting various bits of conduit, none of which were any good, and eventually retired, inevitably, to a bar. When we finally got our *dabdab* and hurried away to find a camp site it was dark and bitterly cold. It was even colder next morning at dawn, yet an early rise was essential to avoid being surrounded by half the villagers in whose surprisingly close proximity we had spent the night. I hadn't come prepared for the cold and felt pathetically ill-clad in shorts and shirt. Hussein, on my advice, had no warm clothes either but he had his own solution. 'A little benzine' he called it, and his dental grin closed around a bottle of wine he had brought from yesterday's bar.

Chewing bread rolls we followed the well-worn trail eastwards. There were no wheel-marks but the impressions of donkey hooves, mule hooves, and the great rounded-heart pads of camels were beaten into every soft spot. The sun soared and grew before us, etching the rocks in brilliant sharpness and throwing broad shadows along the drystone walls. The scene was one of appalling destruction. For the most part there was no vestige of the forest which once clothed the slopes. Scrubby bushes grew along the wayside but within the stone walls there was only a rubble of stones with a little of what passed for soil in between. A boy carried a yoke across his back, his father shouldered a crude plough. Between them a pair of oxen plodded along to the field where, yoked together and hopelessly matched, they would spend another day raking through the stones.

By mid-morning it was the same wherever we looked and would be the same all over the north for it was the ploughing season. Random stone walls divided tiny, fragmented plots where unhappy combinations of oxen dragged a simple, pointed ploughshare and fine-featured, proud-looking men stumbled and staggered along behind, clutching the single beam and shouting direction or perhaps abuse.

The process had been going on for so long that not only were the slopes denuded but even the valley floors had lost their fertility. Sometimes their soil had been completely eroded. Destruction and poverty; poverty and destruction, each now increasing the other.

The sun was warming and the day's traffic was beginning. The first of many caravans filed by. It was a camel train; a string of some fifteen camels tied head to tail, gangling past and peering over the Land-Rover with a strange combination of the nervous and supercilious which camels so often seem to express. Each camel carried some sixteen rectangular blocks about the size of an attaché case.

'*Chew,*' said Hussein. Salt.

I knew what it was though I would not have recognised the grey slabs had I not known. The salt had been hacked out of the old sea bed in the Danakil Depression. The loads were loosely covered with matting, presumably so that they wouldn't dissolve off the animals' backs in a good shower of rain. The camels looked thin and weary.

'How long have they been on the road?' I asked.

Hussein addressed one of the drovers in Amharic and instantly submerged the three of us in a linguistic morass. The camel-man spoke only Tigrean which in its throatiness sounded very like Arabic. At least it did to me but then I was able to listen quite objectively without being distracted by any measure of understanding. Anyway, between English, Tigrean, Amharic and a few words of Arabic we got nowhere.

Hussein looked frustrated. He prided himself, justifiably, on his languages. He was Arussi Galla by birth and upbringing but now lived among the Amharas and spoke their language as his own. His English was appreciable, his Italian good and he even knew a few words of Afar, the language of the Danakil.

'Bloody Tigrean,' he said hotly.

The drover he was trying to talk to was a small, wiry, stubble-faced fellow. There were three others, all in need of a shave, and one of them, who spoke Amharic, sauntered over and chatted for a few minutes. He explained that the salt-run took eight days altogether, from Makelle to Dallol and back, and in Makelle each salt block sold for an Ethiopian dollar, five blocks to the pound sterling. Who did the camels belong to, I asked.

'Rich men in Makelle,' Hussein interpreted. 'These are only the drovers.'

They made their living running the caravans back and forth, up and down from 7,000 feet to below sea-level and back. Then down again.

We were still at that time on a fairly gentle decline, and surrounded by settled farmland, but this did not last, for the scenery changed dramatically. Farmlands came abruptly to an end and we were soon plunging into a zig-zag descent of the escarpment. On the steep face patches of the original forest had persisted. It was a mixture of junipers and gnarled old olive trees – *weira* in Amharic, a valued firewood. By the track there were huge clearings, made and used by the salt caravans for overnight stops. There was scarcely a blade of grass to be seen and I was surprised that the olive trees had sustained the demand for camp fuel as well as they had. One caravan was still in camp, resting. The camels were couched with their loads stacked beside them. The men sat round a fire talking. Another, bigger, caravan came grunting and clattering past with a mixture of camels, mules and donkeys. Two men and a couple of boys walked alongside in silence except for the odd shout and whack at the animals. We pulled out of the way and one of the men stopped to ask for a cigarette. I gave him one. No language problem there, just a puffing sign and a nodded thanks.

I lost count of how many caravans we passed that day, line after line of weary animals and hard, sometimes tired-looking men. We overtook some who were going our way. The rear animals usually carried a few bundles of camping things for the men but most of them were loaded with fodder for the downward journey. It would be finished when they reached the depression and for the return to Makelle there would be only salt to carry and no food.

The junipers and olives petered out as we lost height and the track degenerated into a helter-skelter scree slope as we lurched and slithered through deep, steep gorges of stark rock scattered with *Dracaena* trees looking like stumpy palms with aspidistra leaves. There was no wind now and the heat became oppressive. On this, the steepest and most rugged part of the descent, there was also the stench of decay. Mules, donkeys and camels had all succumbed and the remains ranged from scattered bones which the hyaenas had left, to fresh carcasses not yet torn open by the circling vultures. One tree was festooned with entrails.

No loads had been abandoned. Fragments of rock-salt littered the trail but there were no pieces big enough to be worth strapping on to a pack-saddle. The loads from the dead beasts had presumably been distributed among the rest of the caravan.

The last leg of the descent ran through the twisting gorge of the Ein Alla River, though it was little more than a stream at the time. It was apparently fed by hot springs higher up for the water was much warmer than it should have been. We diverged here from the salt caravans. Their route took a short-cut over the side of the gorge while we splashed along the stream in the bottom. It occurred to me that a heavy storm upstream would be disastrous for there was no way of getting the vehicle above the water line. I had once seen the results of a faraway storm on a lowland river. The flood was audible before it actually appeared. Then a roaring brown mass of stones, branches and turbulent water swept into view and a stream we had just paddled through became an impassable barrier. Nasty thought!

A few boulders, slippery and green with algae, had to be moved but on the whole the stream bed was easier going than the steeper rock section had been. There were even a few stretches of fairly smooth sand and shingle with young *Tamarix* trees whose water-borne seeds had been mixed with the sand and were germinating in hundreds now that the water level had fallen. Three banded plovers ran about and picked between the stones and I stopped for a photograph, screwing on a telephoto lens. Hussein laughed when the little bird ran in too close for the lens I was using and I had to drive away from it to focus. They are pretty little plovers with vermilion eyes and bill, and black and white bands around the chest. Yellow wagtails too were quite common on the stream, but there wasn't much life to be seen and in the hot stillness of the gorge everything was quiet except for the constant murmur of the stream. A troop of hamadryas baboons scampered up the side but as I recall even they were silent and we got none of their barking.

It was towards the end, where the gorge became broader and shallower and footpaths traversed the walls, that we met the first person we had seen that day who was not involved with the salt trade. A young mother was driving a donkey along the path which had now appeared beside the stream. Her baby was slung on her back above a roll of straw matting used for covering Danakil huts. A shawl partly covered her plaited hair and she carried a wooden bowl lavishly decorated with shells to match the necklaces she wore. Her dress was a rough, hessian wrap, ankle-length and tied at the waist. She made a lovely picture and I asked Hussein to see if she minded having a photograph taken. Hussein jumped out and approached the girl with salaams and his broadest grin. I smiled benignly from the driver's seat. She looked apprehensive, as well she might for Hussein had by now donned enormous sun-glasses and a peaked cap. It would be hard for anyone to know quite what to make of him. His cheerful friendly nature came through, though; the two exchanged a few words and Hussein beckoned me over. I got my photograph, put some sweets and bread rolls in her bowl, and we drove on. I would have liked to have been able to talk to her; I never saw another girl in Afar looking much like her or so elaborately decorated. The shells must have come from the Red Sea.

The stream meandered across a flat valley floor and the wheels splashed in and out of the warm water as we followed a straighter course across its bed. A few yards beyond the high-water level an ancient, rusted chassis of a lorry lay propped across two boulders and once again I felt pangs of familiar tension at losing contact with all that was reassuring and having to trust that a single, sadly-beaten vehicle would bring us and everything back again.

The gorge finally opened out, the sides fell away and the stream debouched on to a shingle plain. We had reached the bottom of the escarpment. The map said we were barely a thousand feet above sea-level. The heat of the late afternoon confirmed it. Our clothes stuck to the seats in patches of soaking moisture and shirts dried the instant we took them off.

An old vehicle-track had been more or less cleared of stones and we followed it, looking for a camp site. There was no great vista of the depression into which we were heading. Lava ridges obscured any distant views and the heat-haze would in any case have cut down visibility. I looked at the yellow bristles of grass and the low thorn bushes which here and there offered green leaves but no shade that we could take advantage of. Yet people lived here. Hussein pointed over the baking surface of stones and scrub and told me that the white dots were goats. Through binoculars I picked out two men who were herding them, surely at the very edge of existence.

We camped by a sandy watercourse, or 'nullah', where succulent, grey-green salt bushes grew, and doum-palms with branching trunks. A shallow and improbable pool of brackish water catered for a little flock of sparrow larks, small desert birds which really do look like a cross between a sparrow and a lark.

I had no separate mosquito net and had to put up the tent which had one built in. Hussein did the same. We boiled tea on the gas stove, ate a can of something and crawled into the tents for a night of sweaty, airless discomfort.

Dawn came at 5 a.m. and we were ready for it. The very early hours were the best part of the day, and not only for humans. About three hundred yards from the track, shortly after we got under way, a wild stallion stood watching us. His long ears were pricked, tail switching, all attention concentrated on the jolting, rattling danger which was slowly drawing past.

'Donkey!'

Hussein rapped out the word and flapped his hand in a motion for me to stop. For once I had already seen it. 'Donkey' seemed like an insult. He was quite magnificent. The coat was a uniform greyish-fawn except for black transverse stripes on the legs. It shone as if he had been groomed. He took a few prancing steps towards us, an uncertain mixture of curiosity and fear. Then he swung round and cantered off, pausing twice and turning to face us again before finally disappearing from view.

I put down the binoculars and scribbled a few lines in my note-book. It was not the first Somali wild ass I had seen but he was certainly one of the handsomest. Despite their name they have become very rare in Somalia and probably only survive in any numbers in Afar where there are estimated to be at least 2,000. They can be seen in herds of up to fifty strong but as a rule they run in much smaller groups and are sometimes solitary. They are grazers almost entirely, travelling far to crop the scattered tussocks and pulling what little grass there is from between the stones of the lava flows.

Some months earlier, in central Danakil, a dozen wild asses had had to be caught. On the flat plains, with no stones or gulleys, the asses were relatively easy to catch with a short, fast, hectic chase in a vehicle and a final flip of a noose on a stick. It would have been infinitely more difficult on lava. The problems on that occasion arose later, in the transporting, penning, veterinary examinations and general after-care, but we had skilled men for the operation and there were no mishaps. The asses were eventually flown to Israel for introduction into the Negev Desert.

It is difficult to say whether Somali wild asses are a race of pure wild asses or whether they originated from domestic donkeys which had gone feral. They are certainly very wild and distinctive animals today. The fawnish coat has a pink tinge in some lights and is beautifully smooth. Markings are usually confined to leg stripes though there is frequently a thin, dark line across the withers. Overall, the wild ass is much larger and sleeker than his domestic cousin. But then the latter is not the product of nature's exacting system of selection and rejection, it is the result of man's indiscriminating propagation of docile beasts of burden. The Danakil tribesmen are not entirely blind to this and it is said that they sometimes leave out a female donkey to be served by a wild stallion. No doubt some mixing of wild and domestic stock must have taken place by design or otherwise. The people of Danakil also believe that the fat of wild asses possesses medicinal properties so although they are not hunted for food the asses are persecuted nonetheless.

By midday we had covered a lot of ground, spying from ridges and searching sandy patches and nullahs for animal tracks. We had seen half a dozen Soemmering's gazelle and, in twos and threes, twice as many dorcas gazelle, but no more wild ass. We tottered back down a ridge to the Land-Rover with empty water bottles and trickling faces and groaned in unison at the depressing sight of a totally deflated tyre. Changing the wheel and levering the tyre off and on to mend the puncture was a routine job but it left us both in a state of almost febrile fatigue, limp, wet and shaking. We lay in the strip of shade beside the vehicle and marvelled at the gazelles and asses which lived without shade in this sunken furnace of a desert. The max-min thermometer in the shade beside me did not fall below 120° F. – not an especially hot day by all accounts. During the night it had dropped to 85°F.

'These gazelles drinking?' Hussein asked as he gurgled at the water from the jerry can.

I said I wasn't sure but if they had enough green leaves they probably wouldn't need to. He shook his head incredulously. I would have liked to have gone on to try to explain how they managed it but I didn't think I could cope with the exposition, especially without using technical terms. Indeed, I wasn't altogether certain how they managed it myself. The problem had been intensively studied in camels and it was known that similar processes operated, though not always to the same extent, in other desert mammals including gazelles and donkeys. They are all faced with the same basic problem: the evaporation of moisture causes cooling – but how to afford the moisture when water is scarce or non-existent? Dehydration can be just as lethal as direct overheating. The blood is left thicker and flows less easily. This puts a strain on the heart and the blood doesn't transport the animal's own body-heat to the surface quickly enough for it to dissipate. The animal thus heats up from within and is killed that way.

In desert animals such as camels, asses and gazelles, several factors operate at once to prevent all this happening. The coat is such that it insulates the skin from the sun's rays but at the same time it doesn't impede the evaporation of sweat. Kidneys are powerful enough to be able to concentrate urine and save water that way. The normal body temperature is not as constant as in humans. In camels it occupies a range of eleven degrees or more. At night, for instance, a camel cools down to about 93° F. It can then spend several hours of the next day warming up to about 104° F. before it must start losing water in sweat to prevent further rise. Both camels and donkeys are somehow able to avoid losing water from their blood during dehydration and can tolerate the loss of enormous amounts of water from other tissues and elsewhere – equal to a quarter of the body weight in donkeys, more in camels. In man the limit is about twelve per cent. When they get to water the dehydrated beasts can make good all their losses in one colossal drink.

Birds, too, have to come to terms with the same problem of conserving water while keeping cool. They don't waste much water in excretion, for the urine takes the form of solid uric acid crystals – the white part of a bird's dropping. But by panting to keep cool and rapid breathing during flight they lose water at a serious rate. Because they can fly, nowever, many desert birds are able to feed far from water and still visit it for a drink each day.

Ostriches don't fly. It would be a miracle if they did for a big one can weigh 300 lb. The biggest birds known to have flown in the past weighed a mere 50 lb. and they needed a wingspan of nearly fifteen feet. But because of their size they have a relatively small surface-area through which to lose moisture and gain heat from the sun. They also have some impressive physiological powers; they can certainly do without drinking for several days and can make do with very brackish water when they do drink. Like a camel or a donkey, an ostrich can also withstand the loss of a considerable proportion of its body weight through dehydration if necessary.

We saw ostriches later that afternoon. They were running in a well-spaced line across the horizon as we drove imperceptibly downhill towards the centre of the depression. It put me in mind of Lake Stefanie; the same distorted shapes of the animals and the lack of colour in the grey-brown forms as they rippled across the mirage. Speed seemed to be involved in the illusion too, the blobs were streaking through the haze at an impossible rate and they had vanished by the time we reached the spot. But there was nothing illusory about that.

The edge of the salt flats resembled a vast, disused skating rink, dusty and littered with chunks of black ice. We picked up the path of the salt caravans again and followed it for the last two or three miles to the salt mine. It was a strange sight, the 'mine'. Acres of the salt crust, the floor of the desert, had been smashed up with crowbars and the slabs levered up and left at an angle. Again it looked like an ice surface, this time in the wake of an ice breaker, but some of the pieces had been trimmed into neat rectangles and stacked. Salt blocks had also been used to build a number of small huts in which the salt breakers took shelter from the sun. Two of them came out as they heard us approach. I drove by slowly with a wave and '*Tenastilin*' but got no response.

At the edge of the smashed-up area trains of camels were couched in the sweltering heat, waiting to be loaded. A few mules and donkeys stood about, heads hanging dejectedly. We were 300 feet below sea-level. The drovers must also have been lying in the shade of the little salt huts; I saw only two boys fiddling with the straps of one of the donkeys. Work would resume when the sun was easier to bear.

Still staring at the scene we pulled away from the salt mine and headed further eastwards towards a range of low hills which marked that edge of the salt plain. It was some miles away but judging the distance was difficult. As we left the work site we began to see the salt surface as it was naturally. For hundreds of square miles the great plain was not smooth like an ice rink but was raised into walls about two inches high which formed polygons about three feet across. It looked like an endless pattern of wire netting, or the surface of honeycomb. Only where the raised pattern had been kicked to pieces or flattened down did the surface show any change. Clearly when rain fell into this enormous frying-pan the salt would dissolve and the pattern would disappear. As it dried out again the expanding crystals would once more force up the same pattern. The result, as we crunched across the surface at forty miles an hour, struck Hussein as being quite unearthly.

'Same like the moon,' I heard him remark with his head out of the window.

It certainly wasn't like anything I had seen on earth. At one point brown rocky crags arose from the salt like a terrestrial coral atoll some thirty yards across and twenty feet high. We climbed about on it, bashing bits off. It was all rock salt and, as far as I was concerned, quite inexplicable.

Wheel marks appeared again and we found ourselves on a straight track which was obviously taking us to the Dallol police post – our immediate destination. Both the map and the secretary in Makelle had told us that the outpost was due east of the salt mine, on the low hills which bordered the plain. Just before we got there we passed a derelict building a stone's throw off the track. It looked even more unlikely than the salt atoll. Nothing, as far as one could see in any direction, except a queer surface of sculptured salt and a range of stony hills still a mile or two away. And here was a large building with an iron roof and sides, doors, broken windows and, of all things, a big refrigerator standing outside.

'It's been a proper saltworks.'

'Must have been a rich crazy man,' was Hussein's considered opinion.

We snooped about the place for ten minutes or so with pillage as well as curiosity in mind but there was nothing terribly exciting except that upon a mass of rusted hardware and machinery I discovered an excellent if cumbersome lever for the winch. It was so hot to touch that I dragged it along with the cord on my binoculars. Neither of us could bear to hold it. Before leaving and with heat-demented humour, we made a show of checking that there was nothing in the fridge then slumped back into startlingly hot seats and bowled along to the police station, full of questions.

The track bisected an airstrip near the edge of the plain, just a long strip of gleaming salt with all the raised bits wiped off. A limp wind-sock hung at the side. Four plump, mottled brown birds with yellow throats waddled about on the strip. They were spotted sand-grouse, very much a desert species which often make long, powerful flights each morning to drink. They lay their eggs on the sand and carry water to their young ones, of which there are usually three, until they are able to fly. There appeared to be nothing for these four on the sterile surface but they toddled about quite contentedly while we peered at them. They look like something between a partridge and a pigeon and are zoologically close to the latter.

We had both been wearing sun-glasses over the salt flats. The salt was hardly pristine white, more like a dirty brown, but the glare was intense even so. Glasses came off, however, within moments of our reaching the edge of the plain. In fact it was just as we topped the low, bouldery ridge which bounded it on the eastern side. I knew vaguely what to expect, Hussein evidently didn't, but for the second time that day we were both left mumbling senseless things about the moon.

There were no buildings in view at that point and all about us sulphur had coloured the confusion of rocks to create a weird polychrome landscape of brilliant reds, orange and green. I could not account for how it had happened but the effect was remarkable. We marvelled at it for some minutes. It wasn't just the colours, it was the whole unearthly atmosphere of the place. Nothing, absolutely nothing, moved. There was no bird, no sound, no breeze, no life or movement of any kind; just the still, garish rocks and the endless sea of dry salt beyond.

Ten minutes later we were confronting a road barrier at the police post, and that wasn't quite what I'd expected either. A compound in a natural basin was surrounded by arc-lights and electric cable. A strange steel vessel, like a boiler with pipes coming from it, loomed above us on the left and within the compound we could see tin-roofed sheds. Still nothing moved. I hooted and a man in a string vest and khaki denims came running up to the barrier with a rifle. He looked unfriendly. We '*Tenastilin*'d' and I gave him my letter from Makelle. He took it back into the compound and immediately reappeared and opened the gate. We were met by an unwelcoming sergeant with my letter in his hand.

There were six policemen at the outpost; the sergeant was in charge. They had been sitting on their beds, which were out on a verandah, playing cards. A single police truck was parked in the compound alongside half a dozen rusting, disused lorries. There was a garage at the end of the compound, a row of what looked like abandoned chalets down one side and administrative buildings along the other where the beds were. The sergeant and one other man spoke English but were happier in Amharic. I decided that Hussein was a valuable asset at times like this. He perched on a bed, swinging his legs, and pushed his peaked cap to the back of his head, a little figure with big sun-glasses, a huge grin and an infectious laugh. He had them in such fits with comments about the heat and the moon that I was sorry not to be able to understand them.

A white-skirted Afar chief arrived shortly after us, with two henchmen. They came from an oasis a few miles to the north, virtually on the Eritrean border, as I understood it. I showed them pictures in my African mammals book, keen to know which they would identify. The responses had to be interpreted with caution. All the gazelles occurred in the chief's territory, including the South African springbok! But wild asses were unmistakable, and it was not difficult to guess which of the other animals might be confused with similar beasts. The chief's remarks about numbers seen were worth writing down.

I was not surprised to learn that Dallol was just about the most unpopular of all police outposts but all the rank and file of the provincial force were expected to do a six-month stint there. The sergeant had only thirty-two more days to go; he was marking them off on a calendar. I didn't ask why there was a police post there. It was an open secret that the Eritrean guerillas had been giving the government cause for concern and the Eritrean border was only a few miles away. Men like the Afar chief were probably an excellent source of information in remote areas. The police were in radio contact with Makelle.

The post itself was a disused sulphur works which, according to the police, had been abandoned by an American firm many years earlier. Sleeping in the air-conditioned chalets by day and working by night by the light of the arc-lamps, the enterprising Americans had extracted sulphur and other minerals which were then trucked to the Eritrean post of Massawa. The coloured rocks which we had passed were presumably caused by sulphur particles being scattered by the process; disappointing that what I had taken to be a natural phenomenon turned out to be industrial pollution!

The conversation reverted to Amharic and Hussein took the floor again. I opened a tin of sardines, ate them with dry bread, and wandered off to dispose of the tin. By the side of the garage I lifted a heavy stone and discovered one of my old friends, a fat solifuge. I dropped the stone back and rammed the tin down an adjacent hole.

I suppose we had been at the outpost about an hour and a half. The sun was going down and it occurred to the sergeant to ask where we intended to spend the night. I managed to avoid being pressed into staying and assured the company that I had located a good, safe place about an hour's drive away. There was mild insistence that we stay or at least take a guard.

'The letter says we should help you,' the sergeant said.

I spread my hands expressively and further assured him that they had been most helpful and hospitable. The sergeant seemed satisfied.

'There is one thing though,' I added. 'I've heard about the sulphur springs here. Did we pass them on the way in?'

The sergeant promptly donned a wide-brimmed hat and we climbed aboard the Land-Rover.

We drove through the technicolour landscape into a region where the lava ridges assumed the form of small hills, rather like slag-heaps about ten feet high. I say slag-heaps but they were the most brilliantly-coloured slag-heaps imaginable. In the top of one hill there were pools of lime-green liquid with orange and red crystalline cones protruding above the surface like miniature volcanoes, bubbling out more liquid which cascaded down the hill as a glistening spillway of red, orange, yellow, green and pure white. A similar multi-coloured crust of crystals had formed at the base of the spillway where the solution drained away. Other crystal gardens had arisen on other rock surfaces and all were entirely natural.

It took longer than I'd intended to get the sulphur springs on colour film. The policemen wanted to be photographed against the spillway as a souvenir of their Dallol sentence. Then there were addresses to be exchanged so that I could send the pictures. There was only about an hour and a half of daylight left as we raced back on to the flats, across the airstrip and past the ruined saltworks.

'Saltworks.' I'd forgotten to ask about that.

'Me asking', said Hussein. 'Italian man before working salt.'

I had to be satisfied with that.

The salt diggers were out in force now, toiling among the broken slabs with long levers. The pack animals had mostly gone. We caught up with them later. The camels were linked head to tail following a straight, plodding course for the distant escarpment. On the flat surface their shadows moved with them, perfect, like a film or a silhouette on a desert horizon. The men walked alongside, sticks across their shoulders, their rawhide sandals shuffling on the salt like the great flat pads of their charges. One old man waved to us and we exchanged greetings and gave him cigarettes. His lined mahogany face was weathered and dried by years of scorching sun and salt. Each dark eye glittered from a tight nest of unfathomable wrinkles. The sun no longer burnt, only bathed the scene in a warm light which glowed on the strange earth. There were things I would remember forever about that day.

We left the caravan route and made for the lava ridges which we had passed the day before. I had decided that tonight we would have air.

'Tonight we sleep on top,' I told Hussein. 'More air, very good.'

He nodded and grinned.

Selecting the least steep approach I ground up one of the highest ridges. It was no worse than many of the roads. The ridge levelled out into a flat top about fifteen yards long and ten yards wide. It looked ideal. There was no fuelwood but we could manage with our small gas cooker. The sun had become a diffuse redness in the western sky and the empty quiet of the desert was at the same time tranquil and stirring. We brewed tea and sat to enjoy it. It was a peaceful finish to an exciting day.

The mood changed unexpectedly. A breeze blew up.

'Fantastic, marvellous.'

'Feel that.'

'Sleep like tops tonight.'

The breeze got stronger and the Land-Rover door slammed. It began to whip up dust and grit. We screwed up our eyes. Hussein's hat blew off.

Katabatic effect, I thought, not very helpfully, as we crouched in the lee of the Land-Rover. Sun gone down and the air on the plateau is cooling and rushing down here.

'It'll stop soon,' I assured Hussein.

An hour later, having decided it was bed-time, I waltzed about with my camp bed trying to fit legs on it. Hussein already had his bed up and he weighted it down with stones while he came to my assistance. With the bed put together I rolled out my sleeping-bag as a mattress, flopped on to it and fell asleep in a wind that still seemed to be gaining strength.

It must have been when I went to bury the sardine tin that the dream about solifugids was conceived. It manifested itself, with tactile sensations, at about midnight. The tickling was somewhere behind my left knee. I shot upright to claw at the place and my pillow instantly vanished from beneath me and could be seen, by moonlight, rolling over and over along the ridge.

'Damn!'

I grabbed the plastic jerry can as being the first thing to hand and dumped it on the bed to hold it down while I went to retrieve the pillow. I forgot completely that I'd left the top off the jerry can before going to sleep. Water glug-glugged all over the bed. More and worse curses. In haste I groped for a big stone and hefted it up. It was the one I had used to hold down the screw-top off the jerry can. The tickling, I discovered, was caused by one of the straps of the camp bed lashing against my leg.

Hussein had had a good night, he said next morning.

'Me too,' I lied. It was a calm, merely warm dawn with a sun that seemed to come up almost immediately.

An account of the next two weeks would be mainly a narrative of path-finding. How we spent hours in search of a way round a gulley only to be confronted by a worse obstruction and have to find a way back again; how we spent half a day trying to find a way down into a river bed which matched up with a way out at the other side. How the fuel pump broke and petrol consumption crept up until it doubled before I found the fault, leaving us with fuel supplies to worry about as well.

But we kept going southwards, navigating by compass where necessary, and once we had left the depression the nights were less stifling and there were no more gales. There wasn't much wild-life about either, except for a few gazelles, until we got beyond Lake Julietta. This is a fair-sized lake, about twelve miles long, which must come as quite a surprise if you don't expect it. The water is blue with a border of white foam where the waves lap on the sand and rocks. Doum-palms, weeping *Tamarix* trees and a strange bushy grass called *Aeluropus* fringe the water in a glaucous band between the white spume and the stark rocks which cradle the lake. Clear streams of hot water babble beneath the palms. Small striped fish live there but they never venture into the lake for Julietta is a dead sea, a saturated salt solution.

Travelling through that part of the Danakil was like venturing into a vast, burnt-out forge. Range upon range of raw, scori-aceous lava rose from the desert like immense rakings of cinders. In between, on the flats, the soft, clayey earth lay like brown talc pulverised by hooves and powder-dry. For miles the desert was empty except for the occasional herd of oryx or gazelles. In the thorn thickets one might glimpse a gerenuk or a lesser kudu. The latter were always a thrill; they lack the majesty of their bigger relatives but the white chevrons and flank-markings are more pronounced and they are strikingly handsome. Most of the animals appeared to be in reasonable condition though there was little for them to eat. Only the warthogs were in obviously poor shape and the few we saw, running at a fast trot, tails up like pennants, were thin and ribby. Judging from the recent root-grubbings there were still plenty about, however. They spend much of their time in burrows.

Far to the south of Julietta we crossed from Tigre into Wollo province, though if the map hadn't said so we would not have known. There was virtually no grass to be seen and only the thorny bushes and thickets of acacia bore green leaf. Some of the taller bushes had been hacked down to bring them within reach of the cattle and goats, but now even the goats had moved out and only the signs remained: old thorn zarebas disintegrating into a ring of debris and the spoil of termites, bones, horns and dried fragments of hide scattered by jackals and hyaenas. When we did see stock it was desperately thin. One cow dropped dead literally at our feet as we walked past, selecting a route for the vehicle. Only the goats which thrust into the thorn bushes looked reasonably healthy. Far away to the west the escarpment fell down to the desert in a succession of gentle, cultivated foothills and there, I knew, the crops would have failed again. For this was but the latest of a series of dry years. There were days when we saw not a soul and the only sound was the '*ko-ko-ro ko-ko-ro*' of ring-necked doves. People and stock had gone. Some, who no longer had enough animals to live by, had joined the settled farmers from higher up and sought subsistence in Dessie, the provincial capital. Others who were desperate had made for Bati. Months later Ethiopia's famine was to make world news. It wasn't the first famine and it was hard to believe that it could be the last. In a few good seasons the stock would build up in such numbers that the desert would not support them through the dry years, and dry years there would surely be again.

And yet, amazingly, there were those who looked well-fed and whose stock survived. More likely than not they were the strongest communities – in every sense. They occupied the less-arid stretches along the drainage lines where the bushes were greenest and grass blades could still be extracted from among the low tangle of thorns. We stopped at one such place to ask for a guide, for we had worked ourselves into such difficult terrain that to go on seemed impossible and to go back the way we had come was unthinkable. There were several thorn zarebas, each enclosing a number of the typical domed huts made by laying rush mats over wooden hoops. They looked like old-fashioned bee-hives. A goatskin curtain hung in the entrance hole through which one crawled in and out. The huts were high enough only for kneeling or sitting inside.

We stood outside one of the zarebas while Danakil tribesmen and curious women and children gathered round. As always, every man was armed with at least the traditional heavy knife. Hussein did his bit with a very limited Afar vocabulary and lots of pointing and waving.

'Go big road, Bati–Addis Ababa. No way with car. Go this way? This way? This way?'

Many tribes, perhaps most, would have taken some advantage of our predicament, but not the Danakil. They asked for nothing. A wild-looking youth came forward and said, 'Logia,' with a casual thrust of his chin to the south. He climbed in there and then as if he were going off for half an hour somewhere, and spent the next three days guiding me from one motoring horror to the next.

He was going to Logia, Hussein told me, for the girls. Perhaps the girls in his own settlement wouldn't have anything to do with him. If it was so I could understand it. He was a strange-looking character with a huge mop of fuzzy-wuzzy hair daubed with fat which clung in white blobs and never melted. He patted it now and then, like a woman. I hadn't seen the Danakil men fussing with their hair before, though they sometimes filed their teeth for effect. They did that with slivers of stone and ended up looking like sharks.

We called our guide by a name which Hussein said was an appropriate Afar profanity; he seemed to enjoy being called it. He guided the Land-Rover with camel commands: cries of '*atch*, *aatch*' and such-like for left or right or straight on. I grew very weary of it after a while, and occasionally evil-tempered. It was bad enough crashing backwards down a lava flow without being shouted at. Of course he could have no conception of turning-circles, ground clearances and so on. I was just a poor fool with an ill-disciplined machine.

He was no great problem to cater for, our navigator. At night he just curled up on a groundsheet and went to sleep. He appeared to be quite happy to eat spaghetti and chilli sauce. He drank tea like a camel and smoked all the cigarettes I had left; as a non-smoker I carried them for just such occasions. He got us to Logia on the third day, coming out on to the metalled road within a mile of the village, a glorious race-track mile.

After a plate of fried meat and onions washed down with beer, the squalid little roadside bar in Logia became a first-class hotel. We had more beer, then one for the road. The guide didn't drink and he wanted to be off. I gave him some money and cigarettes which he tucked away in the waist of his cotton skirt. We last saw him, stick across his shoulders, flip-flapping on his clumsy rawhide sandals down a dusty track to the next settlement. He seemed to know exactly where he was going.

We still had some five hundred miles to go to Addis but there was no hurry, and for comparative purposes I intended to spend a day or two in the proposed wild ass reserve of central Danakil. There would be grass there, for like Murlé in the Omo Valley it was a no-man's-land between enemy tribes, this time between the Afars and the Somali-speaking Issas. But the reserve was now bisected by the new Assab–Addis highway and our cross-country problems of the past two weeks were over. Hussein slapped his peaked cap on his knee as we rose to leave, throwing up a cloud of dust. He told me in the friendliest possible manner that next time I went on a cross-country safari he would make sure he was otherwise engaged. I laughed with him but I suspect he meant it.

10

Nomads' Land

Towards the end of the last century Emperor Menelik enormously expanded his Empire by pushing its frontiers into the southern and eastern lowlands. Besides military successes in the south-west, Menelik took the southern Galla country of Borana, and following the conquest of the Muslim kingdom of Harrar in 1887 he penetrated further eastwards into Somali territory. At the same time European colonial powers began laying claim to the Somali country bordering the Indian Ocean. Thus the Somali tribal lands became divided up between Ethiopia, Great Britain, Italy and France. Menelik's share was the vast inland region generally known as Ogaden*, together with adjacent parts of what is now Harrar province.

In 1960 the Somali Republic became independent. It was created from the former British and Italian colonies but the Somalis, having embraced the idea of a Greater Somalia, were far from content to see Ogaden remain Ethiopian. Throughout the fifties and sixties border disputes periodically flared into open warfare and Ogaden remained a prohibited area in which visitors, including itinerant biologists, were not permitted freedom of travel. This regrettable situation lasted until 1968 when a peace treaty was negotiated.

Three years later the Ogaden was reported to be peaceful and restrictions were lifted. It was an opportunity not to be missed. One is naturally keen to see places which have always been out of bounds, and as far as I was concerned the Ogaden was new country and its ecological affinities were with Somalia rather than the rest of lowland Ethiopia. There were thought to be animals there which occurred nowhere else except in Somalia,

* Strictly the region occupied by the Ogaden tribes but used loosely to refer to a much larger area.

dibatag for instance, and beira antelope.

In London the Fauna Preservation Society was also keen to have news from the Ogaden, especially concerning rare species, and they agreed to help out with funds for petrol if I could arrange a trip. A trip was promptly organised. In Addis Ababa I made a phone call to Mike Gilbert, a botany lecturer at the Haile Selassie I University. I told him I was planning a month's tour in the Ogaden and asked if he was interested. The response, I recall, was an explosive and strongly affirmative reply. Mike's special interest was the vegetation of arid regions.

With virtually nothing to go on, I decided that this trip would have to take the form of a general recce. I calculated that there would be well over 1,000 miles of motoring with nowhere to refuel; obviously not a problem which could be solved with a few jerry cans. A visit to the *mercato* was indicated. The Addis Ababa market deals in most lines; those which cannot be displayed can usually be produced upon request, though with second-hand car parts there may be a few days' wait. All I wanted were petrol drums and I found that there was a special department for them. In one ear-splitting alleyway drums by the hundred were being sawn and beaten into dustbins, storage bins, or simply being rolled and kicked about as petrol drums. I bought four forty-gallon ones after some hurried bargaining and managed to get away without having my pockets picked.

We left Addis a few days later with an assurance from the airport that two drums of petrol could be carried by regular air service from Dire Dawa (the last airstrip before Ogaden) to a small town in southern Ogaden called Godé. One drum would be carried in each of our two loaded Land-Rovers and this supply plus the fuel held in the Land-Rover tanks would get us to Godé, by which time the other two drums would have been dropped for us. We were not very happy about the arrangement but we could think of no other way.

There is nothing dramatic in the journey to Dire Dawa unless perhaps the volcanic scenery of the Awash Valley. You take the south road out of Addis, dropping into the rift and turning after forty miles to follow the old French railway which runs to

Djibouti. The traveller by road or rail finds himself, after a couple of hours, slipping eastwards into the Afar Depression, following for a while the course of the Awash River which rises in the highlands west of Addis and ultimately drains into a brackish lake on the French border.

One hundred and thirty miles from Addis both road and rail bisect Ethiopia's first declared National Park – the Awash. It incorporates an old imperial hunting reserve located in a bend of the Awash River. The reserve had ceased to be used as such and had for years been left to look after itself. This it had done with only a poor measure of success. Some animals had disappeared altogether and others were declining in numbers. Then the place came to be threatened with irrigation schemes and agriculture, so in 1966 the newly-established Wildlife Conservation Department took it as a high priority to install a warden and a guard force and declare the area a National Park.

The 350-square-mile park will never be among the world's great game areas but it has its charms and there is probably no better place anywhere to see beisa oryx. At its best there is a quiet, casual air about the Awash park which adds enormously to the pleasure of watching wildlife. I have met the most discriminating people, hardened travellers of Africa, who have thrilled like children to the sight of oryx herds and Soemmering's gazelle on the open grasslands, or the kudu and tiny grey and rufous dikdik which materialise from the thornbush.

The park includes Mount Fantalle, a dormant volcano which is visible from the main road across the blackish jumble of a nineteenth-century lava flow. The lava actually spilled from a smaller crater on the flanks of Fantalle; local folklore dates the eruption at about 1810. In many places hot gas or possibly steam blew enormous bubbles in the cooling lava, some of them fifteen feet or more in height. One of these blisters was very neatly displayed by the railway workers when they cut it in half to let the line pass. Today, apart from a few panting steam vents, Fantalle is quiet and klipspringer and mountain reedbuck live on its caldera walls.

To the serious student of animal behaviour Awash is an

Hamlet in the Simien Mountains

Encounter on the way to Hammer Koké (probably Hammer tribe)

The Danakil guide to Logia – 'going for the girls'

The salt ‘mine’ at Dallol

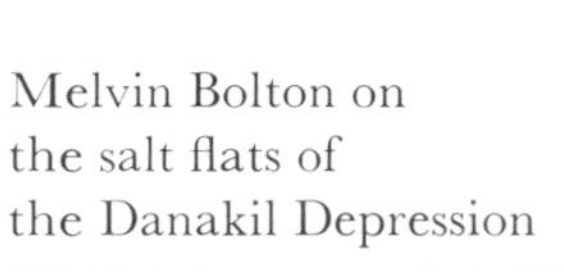

Melvin Bolton on
the salt flats of
the Danakil Depression

especially interesting place for baboons. Both the common olive baboon (*Papio anubis*) and the maned hamadryas (*Papio hamadryas*) live around the Awash River gorge. They hybridise there despite the fact that the two baboon species have entirely different codes of social conduct. Both types live in big groups of about thirty to sixty individuals and in *anubis* society the dominant males challenge each other for reproductive rights to the most desirable of the receptive females. The mature male hamadryas baboons on the other hand each maintain their own private harem of two or three females and their young. The females are expected to know whose harem they belong to and straying wives are likely to be brought home with a powerful bite in the neck.

Should a loose *anubis* female be abducted for a hamadryas's harem (or experimentally forced into that situation by the behavioural scientists who worked all this out) she soon learns how she is expected to behave. It is not in the nature of a male *anubis* however to have anything to do with the business of keeping a harem together and hybrid males are inferior at it in comparison with pure hamadryas individuals. In baboons, it would appear, harem management is an innate aptitude. When you think of it, there must be some interesting case-histories at Awash.

The people we passed looked like Danakil but with bushes of hair smoothly cropped, like topiary or one of those cushion-forming rockery plants. They were Karraiu, a Galla people whose homeland does not extend beyond the throat of the Afar Depression. They show some cultural affinities with the Danakil on whose doorstep they live. In fact the territories of the Danakil and Karraiu meet in the Awash park. Like the Danakil, the Karraiu are nomadic pastoralists; so too are the people of Ogaden and indeed most of lowland Ethiopia, for in the lowlands, only on the western side of the plateau is there enough rain to grow crops. To the north and east and in the lowest country to the south of the highland mass, the annual rainfall is irregular and well below the thirty inches or so necessary to support cultivation away from the rivers.

We purred through the park on the tarmac road which had

brought us comfortably from Addis. Just beyond the park boundary the tarmac ended and we rumbled over the Awash River on a Bailey bridge and entered the province of Harrar in a cloud of dust. There was a choice of roads further on, at a place called Miesso. The direct one followed the railway line and continued along the southern edge of Afar at the foot of the rift wall. The other, better one, climbed the escarpment and ran through the green farmlands of the Chercher range. The high road was said to offer some good views but it was bound to be heavily settled and could present camping problems. Besides, there wasn't much daylight left in which to admire the scenery but we might spot some game on the low road. So we stayed with the dust and later pitched camp behind an impenetrable thicket of prickly pear. I remember it well because before turning in I stood too close to it and got one trouser leg full of minute, irritating bristles.

'Glochids,' Mike said.

I replied appropriately and went to bed.

Dire Dawa grew up as a 'half-way house' on the railway line. With a population of 50,000 it now ranks third among Ethiopian towns. Part of it is Arabic in style and reminded me slightly of Assab. The rest of the city has a European character with avenues of ornamental trees, neat pavements, little villas hiding behind bougainvillaea and an occasional lurid poster advertising the current cinema shows.

We went straight to the airport when we arrived but it was Sunday and there was no one there who could help us. We camped outside town and returned next morning. The man we spoke to had no wish to be difficult, I felt, but it said in his book that petrol could not be carried on passenger planes. He would have to consult the authorities in Addis. Of course I had already consulted them and I tried to telephone the man who had told me there would be no problem, cursing myself for not having insisted on something in writing. By lunchtime I had had no success. Not to worry, they said at Dire Dawa, in the afternoon they would get him by radio.

Mike and I idled away the siesta on a corner balcony outside a bar while my game-guard, Tafera, wandered off somewhere to enquire about watches. The streets were almost deserted. The occasional car went by, or a horse-drawn gharry, and at one point two slender Somali girls flip-flopped down the centre of the road leading a string of gawky camels. There were contraband pedlars hanging about but even they disappeared during the peak lull. It was a lazy, balmy, beery lunchtime.

We sat and strolled around the airport during the afternoon, it came easier than stamping about full of impatience and adrenalin. The man didn't succeed in getting anybody on the radio but we hadn't really expected him to; tomorrow he would try again.

We formed a plan and left for Harrar city which is a little over thirty miles away and some two and a half thousand feet higher on the Eastern Plateau. It was a smooth run, never very steep or particularly exciting scenically. There were tidy little terraces near the top with bushes of chat (*Catha edulis*) growing in rows. The leaves contain a stimulant which is extracted by chewing them for a while. Ethiopia produces an appreciable tonnage of chat, much of it for export through Aden to the Arabian countries.

We passed the turning where we would have come out had we taken the high road from Miesso, then after topping the escarpment we dropped gradually southwards to the provincial capital. There were farms and Galla settlements all the way.

The old city of Harrar is a cramped, pear-shaped little world within a city wall. A brief walk through its warren of narrow, uneven streets leaves one with few clear recollections and a kaleidoscope of impressions: brilliantly coloured fabrics and baskets, tiny shops heavy with incense, sacks of grain, a mosque, whitewashed walls and smelly alleyways, women in shawls and trousers, culs-de-sac and cryptic doorways. There are Arabs, Somalis and Gallas but the real people of Harrar are the descendants of South Arabian colonists who are believed to have settled and established an emirate there more than a thousand years ago. The Hararis speak their own language (*Adari*) and live by their own customs. Harrar baskets, like Jimma stools, have become a special local craft. The women weave them in intricate patterns from coloured straws.

Modern Harrar, with its military academy and provincial government offices, necessarily grew up outside the city wall and has nothing in common with the old town. Next morning, before working hours, we took up positions outside the Governor's office to try to catch him before he became too involved with other matters. A secretary duly arrived and bore off our letters of introduction. We were shown into a side room where a few more petitioners joined us. The place began to take on the strained quiet of a dentist's waiting-room. We found ourselves talking in undertones as we flipped through the dreary literature on the table. The atmosphere was shattered when an immense, obese Somali heaved himself through the door. The room was filled with wheezing and darkness and the thumping of his hefty walking stick (which was dyed to match his hennaed beard) until he subsided into a chair in the centre of the room. Whoever he was, he was a splendid diversion.

A messenger announced that the Governor was ready to see us and minutes later we had made our request. The Governor proved to be all we could have wished for; he was interested. More than that, he actually wanted to help. Yes, he said, there would probably be a police convoy leaving for the Ogaden and he felt sure that they would carry petrol for us. He made a phone call there and then to the chief of police.

'Saturday . . . good . . . benzine, two barrels . . . Mustayel . . . *ishi*.'

So that problem was settled. In the afternoon we delivered the two drums of petrol to police headquarters. Mustayel was before Godé and would do nicely. Furthermore the Governor wasted no time in making out a letter of introduction for each subordinate governor through whose *Awraja* we might want to pass, plus a few extra ones. I collected the letters the same afternoon. There were fourteen of them, all sealed and addressed and bearing a registration number from the archives. We had obviously received priority treatment.

Before leaving Harrar I called the airport at Dire Dawa. Good news, I was told, the authorisation had come through; they could fly our petrol to Godé. I thanked the man for all his trouble and told him it didn't matter any more.

To get to the Ogaden you take the road east out of Harrar. It runs to Hargeisa in Somalia, bridging several sizeable rivers which drain southwards down the long slow dip of the Eastern Plateau. The first ones we crossed were tributaries of the Webi Shebelle which carries fresh water (and a considerable quantity of topsoil) to the Somali coast. The other rivers join the Fafan which peters out finally in the Ogaden. The rocky, scrub-covered ridges and river valleys support an interesting variety of wildlife even though, in the vicinity of the roads and higher up, the valleys are heavily settled and cultivated. Elephants pass up and down these valleys, not in great numbers but enough to cause havoc with the corn. We drove through the village of Babile where nearly a score of game-guards had been assigned the special duty of keeping elephants out of crops. By imperial order the elephants of Harrar were not to be killed. I once saw a herd of forty-two in the Fafan Valley, probably most of the population. They were peacefully browsing on prickly pear.

We stopped for the night at Jigjiga, a smallish town about forty miles from the border and an important market-place for the nomads. There was a reasonable hotel there called 'The Ogaden'. It took most of the following day to get away. There was the Governor to see, a Somali interpreter to be hired and the clutch to be fixed on Mike's Land-Rover. The last job took most of the time, a box spanner had to be adapted to serve as a vital bit of the works.

There are no filling stations after Jigjiga but one does not feel any sense of remoteness in travelling south into the Ogaden; as far as Degahabur at least (a little over 100 miles from Jigjiga), there is a bus service. It was thornbush country and teeming with cows, goats, camels and sheep. A little further east I once visited an open, windswept plain known as Harshin Meda and instead of sheep counted Soemmering's gazelle in hundreds at a time.

From Degahabur, all dust and barracks, to Awari, which I

don't remember much about, and thence to Werder. We camped well away from the roads and used the camps as a base for forays into the surrounding bush. Mike searched diligently for succulents while I recorded what there was to be seen of the animal life. On the road, stops were frequent and we passed each other at fairly short intervals.

Mike, in his normal working posture, usually appeared to have his black beard entangled in a bush, but just before Werder I came upon him standing in the middle of the track making halt signals.

'Dibatag,' he said, with the brevity and the air of one who knows what effect his news will have. 'It ran right across the track in front of me.'

He could not have been mistaken. The name dibatag is a Somali word meaning 'tail erect'. It is a strange and beautiful antelope sometimes called Clarke's gazelle but not really a gazelle at all. Some authorities think it most nearly related to reedbucks. It stands rather less than three feet at the shoulder and, like the gerenuk with which, over part of its range, it shares very similar habitat, it has a disproportionately long neck. Its peculiar characteristic, though, is that it runs with its tail straight up. The occurrence of dibatag in Somalia is quite well documented but practically nothing was known about its status on the Ethiopian side of the border.

I stared at the ground, my feelings an unsettling mixture of excitement at the sighting and frustration at having missed it. In the loose, sandy soil the indistinct prints could easily have been taken for those of gerenuk of which we had seen about half a dozen since Degahabur. They led diagonally across the road and disappeared into vegetation which at that point was too dense to walk through without armour. It was fairly uniform bush of *Acacia, Commiphora* and *Boswellia* with knobbly knots of *Euphorbia* trees poking above; *robecchii*, Mike said it was. There was no hope of following up the dibatag and we decided to push on to Werder and make enquiries there. We had dropped considerably in altitude since Jigjiga; Werder lay around 2,000 feet, which in that part of the interior was low enough to be uncomfortably warm. It was midday as we drove past the row of shops and bars which formed the focal point of the village. There was an open square of bare earth, no grass and little shade. Camels and nomads crowded around a well but there were not many other people about. We made straight for the flagpole which always identifies government buildings. There was a sort of courtyard which apart from a sentry and a tame but unsociable ostrich was deserted. With statesman-like decisiveness we returned to the bars.

At this point a Land-Rover drew up and we were confronted by Major Alemayu, chief of the Werder police. The Governor was away in Addis, he told us, and he was in charge. I extracted the appropriate letter from my batch and handed it to him with a growing feeling that we were going to have trouble. For perhaps half an hour we practised courteous, verbal manœuvres around an outstretched map on the Land-Rover bonnet.

Our letter said we were on official business and should be offered every assistance. The major therefore considered himself duty-bound to provide a police escort but as his truckload of constables were all away we would have to wait in Werder for a day or two until they came back. It was a familiar situation. If you don't produce a *dabdab* you run the risk of being stopped for travelling in remote areas without authorisation. If you do have the necessary letters you are likely to get VIP treatment and get lumbered with a police escort. I have nothing against escorts in principle but in practice they are an unbearable imposition. Generally I could demonstrate that there was no room in the Land-Rover and since the police could rarely provide transport of their own, the problem usually resolved itself. But Major Alemayu was threatening to send a veritable troop truck. We would be rushed safely from one village or police post to the next and followed about by guns and chatter whenever we walked off the road.

People were gathering and I set our Somali interpreter to enquiring about dibatag. The major, who was less than entranced by the subject of dibatag distribution, suggested that we continue our conversation in more comfortable surroundings and led us to a bar with a paraffin fridge.

As the afternoon wore on and the empties accumulated in the sand at our feet the tone of our meeting became what might have been officially described as 'cordial'. We became the major's confidants, up to a point. His biggest problem, he confessed, was not bandits or cut-throats but smugglers.

'Every time they are passing by a different way,' he complained. 'They have their own roads, you know; they go with camels and sometimes trucks. Even now my men are on patrol but they cannot be everywhere at once.'

We nodded sympathetically. As for contraband; since Dire Dawa we had been offered cigarettes, watches and revolvers without our having shown any acquisitive interest. They just happened to be things which easily went out of sight under Somali skirts and could be produced in seconds for a quick sale. These and other items were also available in bulk and one got the impression that the thornbush must conceal whole chains of supermarkets.

From smuggling to poaching and from poaching to dibatag and back to the question in hand. Local informants maintained that the animals were most plentiful further east, near the border around a place called Galadi. So in the late afternoon, with troop trucks forgotten, we took our leave of the sad-eyed major and drove, while we still could, eastwards.

The country offered no change in scenery. We had been on red sand since Awari and it was now so loose that in places it was hard to keep going. There were camels or signs of camels just about everywhere and the previous day I had come to appreciate that the term 'ship of the desert' is more fitting than is generally realised. We had witnessed a nomadic family moving house. Like the Danakil they used a combination of grass mats and curved wooden poles to build huts which could be dismantled and carried on camel-back. What I had seen over the tops of the bushes were the bundles of bows curving fore and aft into the air and rocking the loads which they cradled, quite astonishingly like boats pitching on a grey-green sea.

We saw four more dibatag next morning, still only fifty miles from Werder. They walked casually out on to the track ahead of us, then bolted into the thornbush. I didn't get a proper look at them as they had been against the sun and several hundred yards away but there was no second chance. They had gone and they were not to be relocated.

At Galadi we found the Governor, *Balambaras* Ayele, at home, cleaning a rifle. He was at once friendly and hospitable and took no exception to being disturbed on a Sunday morning. The English, he believed, were not such a bad lot. By the early evening we were on a stony road south being guided to the best place for dibatag that the local Somalis could think of. Our guides were two minor chiefs of the district, or so we were told. Whoever they were, the chief of police in Galadi had been adamant that they accompany us for our own safety, and the *Balambaras* believed that the policeman knew best. I had wanted to go further east to look for beira but that had been out of the question.

Before long the bush began to thin out and we were soon driving across plains of low shrubs with sparse grass and a scattering of acacia trees and bushes. Visibility was quite good but we drove until sunset without seeing any game and our Somali companions were plainly perplexed.

While the tents were being put up one of them squatted on a low termite mound and stared intently into the failing light. He was a thin man with a prominent Adam's apple. Hooded, half-closed eyes with sweeping lashes peered down a long, broad nose. In profile he looked like a camel. Jumping down off his pedestal he indicated that we should walk over to investigate a belt of thicker cover about half a mile away. As we approached it one of the Somalis suddenly raised his arm and pointed excitedly ahead. I followed his gaze and saw nothing. Then, through binoculars, I picked out what he had seen. Three dibatag were standing like statues, watching us. They were a long way off and the light was dim but all the same it was the longest look at dibatag that I ever got. They were slender and graceful, very much like gerenuk but with a heavy black tail reaching down to the hocks. The gazelle-like face markings were not visible.

The next morning I saw six. When I first caught sight of them they were already galloping in single file for the horizon as if they expected to be shot on the instant. In the daylight they were ash-grey with whitish bellies and buttocks. They moved with a curious rocking-horse gait and their black tails wagged back and forth for they carried them stiffly erect as they ran, like beagles. They were easily distinguishable as a male and five females; the male carries horns which, like those of the reed-buck, curve forwards at the tips. I saw another one during the day, and a flock of ostrich.

On the way back to camp I noticed a number of small craters in the ground, one of which was puffing out sand like a tiny volcano. Within it I caught a glimpse of one of the most remarkable and ugliest of mammals. It was a rodent and was adapted in the extreme to life underground. A few white and wispy hairs adorn an otherwise pink and naked body. A slightly raised ring of skin is all that remains to surround the orifice of each ear. The top incisor teeth protrude forwards through the upper lip and little pinprick eyes squint feebly. The naked mole-rat (*Heterocephalus glaber*) looks like a deformed outcast from a litter of premature dachshunds. Digging with their teeth (which they can do with closed mouths) these five-inch sand puppies burrow in the hot dry deserts of Somalia and the adjacent parts of Ethiopia and Kenya. Feeding on roots and succulent tubers they show themselves infrequently but sometimes wander on the surface after dark. That sandy shrubbery near Galadi was the only place I ever saw them.

When I got back to the camp the Somalis were complaining loudly about being kept away so long. They had done what had been asked of them, showed us the dibatag, and now they wanted to go home. On the way back I asked about other animals in the area. None; only aardvark (ant bears). It was likely that large areas of the uniform, waterless bush had never supported a great variety of game animals, but a number of the animals which did occur, including dibatag, should certainly have been more plentiful than we found them to be.

It was the same old story; most people we spoke to considered that edible animals or those with saleable skins were there to be shot.

'If I don't shoot it someone else will,' they would say with simple but disconcertingly veracious logic.

The years of human conflict in the Ogaden might have had one slightly beneficial effect: the Ogaden is the only part of Ethiopia where I did not see firearms being openly carried by tribesmen. In fact we saw only one Somali rifleman during the whole tour and he was running like a hare in a fluster of skirts. But it probably only meant that they kept well clear of the roads. In any case the hunting members of the armed forces could compensate for any fall-off in shooting by the locals.

Our route took us once more through Werder then westwards towards Kebre Dahar. The soft red sands gave way to browner earth and the vegetation changed a little in response to the soil and the slightly higher rainfall. But it was still thornbush, with the same few genera of plants taking up most of the space. One might travel from the eastern Ogaden, across southern Ethiopia almost to Lake Stefanie with no great change in the scenery. It is all camel country; nomads' land. At ground level the withered shrubs, herbs and grasses grew patchily between the thorns. We passed places where localised showers had produced a discernible flush of green but I don't recall that Mike encountered very much in flower. Plants which live where rainfall is slight, and worse still, irregular in occurrence, have to be opportunists and travelling botanists need to be lucky. There are desert plants such as the creeping *Tribulus* (whose little spiky fruits are agony on bare feet), which are able to grow from seeds to blooms and themselves produce fruits all in about three weeks. And the seeds, if need be, can stay viable through years of drought. Some desert grasses will complete their life cycle, from seed germination to seed production, in less than a month and another creeping herb, *Boerhavia repens*, has, amazingly, been recorded to produce seed only ten days after germination.

Before Kebre Dahar we crossed the Fafan River, now just a series of muddy water-holes but enough to meet the water requirements of a devastating number of domestic animals. The surrounding plains, the plains of Korahe, were virtually devoid of vegetation. We coughed our way through the depressing scene in thick choking dust, stopping now and then to count a few Soemmering's gazelle fleeing for their lives.

Nomadic pastoralism is not, in principle, destructive but it is despite the privations an extravagant form of land use. The diet of the nomads varies somewhat with different tribes and depends to some extent on what is available locally. The tribes of central Danakil for instance must depend almost exclusively on milk and what they can make from it. But in general the staple is milk, milk products and meat supplemented with bush fruits and some grain as available. On the basis of a mainly milk diet with perhaps 25 per cent meat over a long period, it has been shown that a family of five (the average family is probably bigger than this) will need to keep about twenty-five cows, or as it works in practice, the equivalent weight of mixed animals – cows, goats, sheep and camels. In an area like Korahe with an irregular twelve inches of rain a year, such a family herd will require over 500 acres of grazing. This in turn limits the human population density to six people to the square mile.

I didn't spend long enough at Korahe to be able to say whether there were too many people struggling to keep enough cattle for their needs or whether less people were trying to keep far too many cows. Both situations produce the same effect on the land but the former state of affairs is not so easy to cure. Around the Rift Valley lakes the Galla took to cultivating, but for them the way out was easy for they had enough rain. In the arid regions the nomads may ultimately have to raise cattle for beef and sell them or exchange them for grain to a far greater extent than they do at present. That way they will not need to keep so many cows. Alternatively, irrigation schemes might provide the answer for some.

Kebre Dahar is an *Awraja* capital. We had a long chat there with its Governor, a colonel, on his verandah and were introduced to yet another police chief. Once again the business about escorts came up. We said as tactfully as possible that we would rather do without. The colonel shrugged and wished us luck. We sped away.

Nearly every day it was necessary to spend some time mending punctures. Young thorn bushes were sprouting vigorously all over the roads. We were thus occupied, applying patches to inner tubes which were already knobbly with them, in a secluded spot off the road a few miles south of a village called Shilavo, when there was the sound of trucks. We looked up, and moments later found ourselves staring into the barrels of rifles and sub-machine guns. It was all very dramatic but turned out to be only the police convoy on its way to Mustayel. The armed guards, having seen our Land-Rovers from their elevated position on the trucks, had with unfailing military instinct surrounded us. There was laughter all round, with a falsetto note of relief on our part, and the convoy raced away again to carry its supplies and our petrol to Mustayel.

The previous evening we had seen three more dibatag, bringing the total to twenty-one individuals sighted. It seemed to be worth spending a day or two in the area but we saw no more dibatag for the rest of the trip.

The Ogaden birdlife was surprisingly rich in variety but, as is so often the case, there were a few species which seemed to be with us the whole time. I came to look upon them almost as companions during the hours at the steering wheel. Some, like the red-billed and yellow-billed hornbills, were conspicuous rather than anything else. Others, like the golden-breasted starlings, were gorgeously colourful. Some were curious; the white-bellied go-away bird earned its ridiculous name by shouting 'go-awaaaa' like some character from a Punch and Judy show.

It was a dusty drive to Mustayel. The soft clay, pulverised by wheels and hooves, came belching in thick clouds through every crevice. We stopped for a couple of days among stony hills. Mike combed the scrub and scree for plants while I tramped about the district in search of animals. It was the first place we had seen which might conceivably hold beira antelope. I asked several locals but the name beira (a Somali word) was not familiar. I saw gerenuk, lesser kudu and numbers of dikdik – but no beira.

Mike had better luck. He strode into camp from the nearest hillside and dumped what looked like two pebbles on the Land-Rover bonnet. '*Pseudolithos*,' he said as calmly as he could. The 'false stones' were rare and little-known succulents which, as far as Mike was concerned, made the whole trip an outstanding success. He had not by that time discovered his most exciting specimen, a plant which was eventually made known to the botanical world for the first time under the name *Euphorbia piscidermis*.

It was the same day, I believe, that we had trouble with bees. Whenever a drop of moisture was uncovered, they settled on it in hundreds. We had to gather up the jerry can and toilet things, sprint to the far side of the clearing and sponge down frenziedly before they found us. We tried to confuse them by running from one side to the other and leaving wet patches about as decoys, but there were just too many bees. Some things we could only do after dark.

Mustayel was on the Webi Shebelle. It wasn't much of a place and we collected our petrol and camped a few miles out of town. The river was properly bridged and our road continued on the other side. I took a long detour, more by accident than design, which looped southwards through dreadfully overgrazed bush. I saw oryx there for the first time since leaving the Awash Valley. Mike and I met again at Kelafo where we fell gluttonously upon a bowl of mutton *wott* before recrossing the river.

Official anxiety about travelling was less apparent as we drew further away from the Somali border and we had no further trouble in declining offers of escorts. For about sixty miles our road clung to the vicinity of the river. I think we had all been harbouring thoughts of a lazy day spent fishing while our washing dried, but somehow it never seemed convenient. The water was muddy and the approaches were either cultivated or busy with stock and herdsmen from the adjacent plains. Mike started to reconsider his dirty linen, unable to think how he ever decided it was dirty, and I adopted a steady-state theory that the point would be reached when dust would fall off my clothes as fast as it accumulated.

At Godé we left the river, by no means reluctantly, and turned north towards Danan. The idea was to continue to Imi on the border of Bale province but that plan didn't work out either; before we reached Danan my Land-Rover chassis broke. It wasn't such a bad track but the clayey earth was baked hard and the bumps and holes probably just finished off a job which some other road had started, possibly months before. I splinted up the fracture with a tyre-lever and wire and took a direct route back to Kebre Dahar. Mike tailed me. Having already met the police chief I sought help at the police HQ and was not disappointed. A mechanic did the welding job the same afternoon but it was hard to say whether the weld would stand up to a battering in the hilly country further west. I decided not to risk it.

11

In Search of Beira

It would seem reasonable to expect that after an arduous safari one would be extra-appreciative of everyday comforts: baths, a soft bed and food which doesn't come out of a can. But it isn't necessarily like that. Sometimes it takes a few days to settle down; you find yourself in the wrong gear, still waking up at dawn and then spending the day pacing about the office unable to sit and concentrate on report writing.

We had been in the Ogaden for only three weeks. I had found no trace of beira and had actually come back with fuel to spare. I found myself repeatedly staring at the maps. If only we could have got east of Galadi. There were hills there according to the cartographers; it might have been ideal country for beira. As it was, no one could even say whether the animal existed in Ethiopia at all. The Red Data Book listed its distribution as the lower hills of the northern part of Somalia, with a few in the small gypsum hills of south-east Somalia. The book also mentioned that they were difficult animals to see, even in the open at a hundred yards. But the fact remained that beira had been recorded in Ethiopia – once. In 1899 P. H. G. Powell-Cotton shot four specimens at a place called Arroweina. His friends in the hunting party shot another three.

Arroweina was somewhere near the Somali border, just south of French Somaliland, but in the general vicinity on the map there was a 'Qawraweina', a 'Weine', a 'Harraua' and a river called Arroweina. Considering that all the names had been written phonetically from the Somali it was a bit uncertain. Perhaps Arroweina had been a hamlet, an ephemeral little settlement now forgotten like hundreds of other places, mapped only thirty years ago. It would take many weeks to investigate the whole area and I hadn't got that much time.

At the British Embassy, it took them only minutes to produce a copy of Powell-Cotton's book.* It was too good to be true. At the back of the book, in a pocket, there was a map showing the route the author had taken through Abyssinia. There was Arroweina, its position fixed by nothing less durable than the mountains. Two days later I was once again in Dire Dawa.

When, a month before, the Provincial Governor had presented me with a fistful of *dabdabs*, he had generously written one to the Governor of every *Awraja* in Harrar, not just the Ogaden region. This meant that I had an unused letter addressed to the Governor in Dire Dawa. I presented it as soon as I arrived and hoped for the best. I had originally sought permission to travel in the Ogaden and was now trying to use the same authorisation a month later to visit a place in eastern Afar more than 200 miles further north. Once in Gemu Gofa, on a foot safari in pouring rain, I was turned back by police because my letter of authorisation was one week old and, by the Ethiopian calendar, was no longer dated for the current month.

The Governor read my letter and I watched his face for expression.

'The place you want to go to now is in the district of Aysha,' he said at length.

'I believe it is, yes.'

'Well the Governor there has been expecting you for some days.'

'Expecting me?' I said lamely.

'Why yes, it must be nearly two weeks since we had word you were coming.'

I said something about mechanical trouble, expressed sincere gratitude and scuttled off to find an interpreter while a new *dabdab* was being prepared.

By the evening I hadn't found anyone who would act as an interpreter for the wages I was able to offer. But the way my luck was running I decided I could manage the trip without one and had not quite changed my mind again by the time I found

* *A Sporting Trip through Abyssinia* by P. H. G. Powell-Cotton, published by Rowland Ward, Ltd, London, 1902.

the right road out of Dire Dawa.

That night I pitched a lonely tent after dark and cooked supper without showing light. I was probably in no more danger from the Issas, the Somali tribe whose territory includes eastern Afar, than I would have been from the Danakil who are their traditional enemies further west. But the Issas were less familiar to me and I had heard some nasty stories.

It was a disturbed night. First I awoke to hear soft sounds coming from near the Land-Rover. I peered out into the moonlight and made out the form of an uncommonly large hyaena, standing with its head resting on the Land-Rover bonnet and sniffing the washing-up which I had left there until morning. Then there was the nightly gong of the petrol drum as the air cooled and the top caved in. Some time in the early hours I was awakened again to find that the sky had blackened and a storm was gathering. I didn't get much more sleep and was glad to be on my way when daylight came.

The rain had stopped by dawn and the early sunshine was bright and cheering without being oppressive. For a while moisture sparkled on the grim wilderness of thorns and rock, and on the stark ruin of an old Italian encampment a little way off. The sticky soil held puddles where birds drank and splashed and for an hour or two the desert's countenance was strangely softened.

I saw a wildcat on the track that morning and eight gerenuk in a single group. I also noted down a pair of African hawk-eagles but I well remember them without consulting the notebook. They are not birds which one sees every day and they are strikingly handsome; almost black above and barred with white and black below, like a giant sparrowhawk. They looked every inch the hunters that they are. Ethiopia must be one of the very best places in the world for birds of prey. Every type of habitat is available and the land is still virtually free of contamination with agricultural chemicals. It is disturbing though to think how vulnerable the raptors are, for it does not matter how impregnable the falcon's eyrie is, if her prey is poisoned with pesticides and the eggs she lays are sterile.

I had to present my pass at a police post about 80 miles from Dire Dawa but they dragged the barrier away without any argument. The track at that point had left the lava flows for smoother ground and was heading towards a group of low, scrub-covered hills. I spent a few minutes enquiring about wild-life; the police, mildly curious, questioned some Issa boys but nothing interesting came of it. The rest of the way to Aysha led through flat, gravelly desert where thousands of black-faced sheep worked meticulously over the scattering of tussocks and shrubs and the occasional locust was driven in an unending series of brief, headlong flights from one quiet spot to the next.

They were the colourful desert locusts of both Asia and Africa. The locusts of legend, of famine and of frustratingly unpredict-able habits from the point of view of pest control. Locusts are not unique among grasshoppers in showing gregarious behaviour, but no other grasshoppers practise it to such a spectacular degree. They fly together in thousands of millions, each million weighing about two tons. So different are locusts in the solitary and gregarious phases that for years they were thought to be different insects. A large proportion of the truth about them was worked out in London, at the Anti-Locust Research Centre. It turned out to be the physical effects of overcrowding among locusts which caused them to change from solitary grasshoppers to flying swarms. Experimentally, overcrowding in cages or even nudging one about continually in a box will cause the crowding instinct to appear, but some of the physical changes take place cumula-tively, over several generations. It is as if the desert locust lives in a constant state of change.

Accepting that gregarious locusts like to be together, what makes them take off in swarms? No one really knows the answer to this one, but it isn't just a case of moving on when the food runs out. Only well-fed locusts could fly as they do on migration anyway, at about ten miles an hour for anything up to twenty hours at a stretch. Swarming disperses the locusts of course, but at the same time the survivors of a swarm tend to get carried by wind into the same general area and so another overcrowding situation is started. Areas where winds converge are often rainfall regions too, and that is exactly what is required for locust breeding. The eggs are laid in the soil which needs to be moist if they are to hatch.

Locusts of every species are an important link in the food chains of animals of savanna and semi-desert country. We observed a kestrel feeding on them that morning on the last stretch of our journey to Aysha.

Aysha lies on the railway line from Djibouti in French Somaliland. It is an unusual village, most of the houses being built from volcanic boulders so that you walk through narrow passages between irregular drystone walls. There were sandal-makers squatting in the shade stitching rawhide sandals which, with casual use, would probably last a lifetime. There were poky little bars and eating houses which stank of paraffin, not so much from the lamps as from the tables which were swabbed down with the liquid to keep flies off. I met a young schoolteacher, Ato Mitiku, who helped me out a good deal. He came to the Governor's office to interpret since the *Wereda* Governor spoke no English.

The Governor was indeed expecting me, or rather he was expecting an expedition, but he appeared to be quite content to accept a loner. The initial response to my enquiries about beira was, to say the least, discouraging. No one, including a number of Somalis in the office, knew what I was talking about.

'Beira, baira, baera,' I persisted, hoping to hit it in Somali, 'like a big dikdik.' Blank faces.

'Have you no pictures?' asked the schoolmaster. I hadn't. The Governor sent out for the local 'wildlife experts'.

Aysha did not appear on Powell-Cotton's map but I estimated that it was not more than about 20 miles from Arroweina. I wanted to hear where the locals thought there were beira before I came up with my own suggestions. A wildlife expert duly arrived, breathlessly and pleasantly aware of his importance like the only boy in the school who can climb through the window when the master has lost his key. I repeated the interrogation and this time there was an immediate reaction. The expert crouched down and held his hands up like ears. That was it; the specific name for beira is *megalotis* – big ears.

'Where?'

'Bio Anot.'

'Never heard of it, where is it near?'

'Marmar, near Marmar,' he said.

Marmar was the name of the mountain range where Powell-Cotton had shot his specimens. I set my fist on the table to represent the mountains and invited someone to show me Bio Anot. One of the Somalis put his finger hard against the base of my thumb.

'Near Arroweina?' I said. He looked at me with a sort of amused amazement.

'Yes, near Arroweina.'

There was a warrantable fuss about going so close to the Somali border but the Governor supplied me with two guides cum guardians and we reached Bio Anot the same afternoon. It was just a police outpost with the huts grouped inside a thorn zareba at the foot of the Marmar range. Between the outpost and the mountains, really the south-east wall of the Afar Depression, there was a wide, dry, sandy river bed. I re-read the notes which I had copied from Powell-Cotton. They ran thus:

> We had decided to remain a couple of days at Arroweina, as the camels were much exhausted and needed a rest; so next morning we all struck off in different directions to look for game. I climbed the cliff 1,500 feet high, just opposite camp, by the dry bed of a torrent . . . Near the summit I spotted, through the glasses, a couple of beasts which I could not identify. Ali said they were beira . . . Taking aim, I dropped the first through the shoulder, hit another rather far back, and with a long shot bagged a third. They proved to be beira, but two of them were females. The horns are thin and scarcely noticeable at a little distance . . . A little later, one of my men reported a couple of beira close by; after a short stalk I found the male lying down, and dropped him as he stood up to look at us.

There it was, the dry bed of the torrent, a broad lane of pale, shining sand. There was the cliff, rising from the nullah in tumbling slopes of broken rock. Arroweina, I gathered, was simply the local name for that section of the watercourse.

The sun was still high and hot as we trudged over the crusted, channelled sand of the river bed. Something scampered beneath the trash which had gathered against a boulder during the last spate. A few small unobtrusive birds flew among the shrubs, a camel, unattended, stood motionless; it was not a time for great activity.

We had driven a mile or two from Bio Anot and had parked the Land-Rover beside some drooping *Tamarix* trees, leaving one Somali squatting by the side of it as a guard. Even by the river shade was limited. The riverside vegetation consisted largely of low, richly-green *Cadaba* bushes and the spindly stalks of *Calotropis*, a cabbagy-leaved shrub whose fruits have the form of inflated bladders. Wrinkled and unripe they look faintly obscene, like monstrous testicles.

My guide was leading me to a mountain footpath and I decided that I knew a lot of Amharic when I came to try to communicate with him for he knew none. I think 'beira' was the only word we had in common. Even sign language failed. Brow-mopping signs were taken to mean 'headache' instead of 'hot' and I was offered an aspirin wrapped in a bit of paper. Somalis, it seems, indicate the heat by flicking a finger beneath the chin. I suppose it's a relative thing; a Somali doesn't consider it hot until the sweat drips off his chin.

We toiled up the mountain path and over broad, scrub-scattered ridges of shattered rock. For two hours we combed those torrid hills, visually quartering the ground from the high points and spying expectantly into the hollows. But we saw nothing except a striped hyaena which was flushed sleepily from its den in the rocks. There was a lanky Somali youth with a herd of goats whom my guide obviously knew. They talked for a while about what we were after, and judging from the pointing and arm waving they knew what they were talking about, but by that time the day was over and whatever they were planning would have to wait until tomorrow.

By about 2 a.m. I still hadn't got to sleep. At the outpost the policemen on night guard had been jabbering furiously since dark and the dogs had probably been barking non-stop since their voices broke, but you don't notice it during the day. I wandered out under the stars (which drove the dogs berserk) and tried to savour the night air. Beneath a tree my guides slept like babies. I had provided them with safari beds but they had agreed to use them only when I took the legs off and laid the canvas on the ground. Apparently they could only sleep curled up and the beds weren't wide enough for curling.

Beyond the thorn barrier, the mountains loomed as a featureless black mass. Up there it would be still and quiet. No lunatic dogs or garrulous policemen; perhaps a slight breeze and the gentle hooting of owls. But the guides and the police had united in insisting that we slept within the compound. I crawled back into bed and downed a draught of whisky which, for one who prefers beer, would normally have lasted half a week. When I came round, with a surprisingly clear head, it was time to get up.

The guides changed duties that morning and I was escorted by the one who had guarded the Land-Rover the previous day. We made a short detour from the path and arrived at the home of the youth we had met the evening before. He shouldered his stick and came with us. We followed much the same course as before, the youth ranging ahead and occasionally disappearing for a while then suddenly popping up beside us and always with a casual, detached sort of air. He obviously knew the mountains like his own back garden, every crevice. He never spoke unless he was questioned.

We sat for a while in the shade of a *Dracaena* tree at the top of a cliff, the guide squinted hopefully around, shading his eyes with his hand, and I systematically scanned the ground below through binoculars. Anything less than scrutiny would have been pointless. The entire surface of the mountain was a mosaic of totally irregular shapes in a confusion of browns, greys and greens white-splashed and dotted with lichens and fragments of limestone. The texture was further complicated by the extremes of brightness and shadow. I was intrigued to know what the youth could see with his steady, sweeping gaze. I couldn't decide whether to regard him as a hawk-eyed master of mountain lore or just a chap who wasn't trying very hard, like those admirably strong, silent types who sometimes turn out to be just a bit slow-witted. As it was, none of us saw any animals, though there were hamadryas baboons barking somewhere at the foot of the cliff.

By sheer good luck, it was I who saw the beira first. We had fanned out on an incline which on my line of travel led up to the lip of a shallow basin a few hundred yards across. As I stared into the depression, five animals clicked into shape and focus. 'Easily mistaken for klipspringer', I had read somewhere; an unsettling phrase at the time for it would be frustrating in the extreme to have a fleeting glimpse of an animal and then not be sure whether it was a common klipspringer or something to get excited about. In full view, these animals were quite unlike anything I had ever seen. 'Giant dikdik' conveys the best impression but they were beira and were as distinctive, unmistakable and delicately beautiful as I could ever have wished.

They had enormous ears, rufous-fawn like the face and limbs, and white-encircled eyes. The back and upper flanks were shining silver-grey but changed with the light. A narrow blackish flank stripe like that of a gazelle bordered the whitish underparts. The animals moved slowly and nervously, in a little herd. The camouflage effect of their colouring was extraordinary; ears and legs flickered and vanished against the sand-coloured rocks while the outlines of their little bodies melted and fused in a moving, changing collage of colour, form and shadow. When the beira stood still they instantly disappeared without any cover at all.

Camouflage is common enough among mammals but I have never seen it work anything like so effectively in the open and with a moving animal. It is a behavioural characteristic of beira that they tend to cling to a small home range, a particular hill or, as in this case, one section of a bigger hill. So it seems reasonable that beira should have better camouflage than, say,

Soemmering's gazelle which inhabit open places where they can and do outrun their enemies. But it is also worth remembering that predators of the larger mammals are mainly other mammals, and among mammals, as far as we can tell, all but the primates are colour-blind. The eye-catching hindquarters of a Soemmering's gazelle may not appear quite so conspicuous through the eyes of a cheetah. Conversely, for what the observation is worth, I cannot say that with my eyes I find beira any easier to pick out on a black and white print than I do in colour.

With hands far too unsteady for the big lens they were holding, I had taken several blurred pictures before my guide arrived at the scene and began shouting and pointing to draw my attention to the animals I was photographing. With hoarse whistles of alarm, the beira bolted. At speed there were moments when the dark flank band was the most conspicuous feature, a questing missile twisting and hovering above the debris. I had a fleeting impression of tropical fish in a tank when dissociated stripes sometimes wriggle and dart across the gravel. I felt sure that they wouldn't have gone very far and we split up and began to search separate sections of the hills.

In the interests of objectivity, it must be said that the colours of beira are as described above but at close quarters, on the museum bench, the grey of the back is said to have a pinkish suffusion and the white of the underparts is said to be tinged with fawn. In the field, with the play of light on the living animal, such subtle tones are lost in the effects which they undoubtedly help to produce. Beira stand about 22 inches at the shoulder and weigh something in the region of 25 pounds. The tail is very short and bushy and the horns are straight slender spikes found only in the male. It is an animal apart, a little antelope of the genus *Dorcatragus*, species *megalotis*. But there are no other species of *Dorcatragus*, it is monotypic. One of its distinguishing characteristics, zoologically, is the presence of a gristly pad on the underside of each hoof. They ought to be able to run silently as a result but as I watched my herd disappearing up the far side of the hollow, I followed their progress more by the clatter of the loose stones than by sight.

On that kind of surface cushioned hooves might help traction but they don't make a great difference to the noise level.

No one really knows very much about beira. Since they were first described in 1894 they appear to have been scarce and only found in small, isolated groups each of which occupies its own particular hill. Half a dozen questions spring to mind at once: Do they have a definite breeding season (both Powell-Cotton's female specimens were pregnant)? Do they actually defend territories against rivals? If they have territories, would they, like grouse on a moor, be content with smaller territories if the food supply were increased? Just what is important to them, and within a reserve what more could be done to increase their density? They evidently don't need to drink.

For many African game animals basic questions of this sort can now be answered, but with the beira antelope all is a mystery. It is not just an academic mystery either. Specific conservation measures have to be tailored to the requirements of the animals and until these are known it is not always easy to decide what to do for the best. For someone who can devote the time to it, finding out about beira can hardly fail to be a fascinating project.

It was the youth who found them, after about two hours. He came up to me and beckoned in such an offhand way that I thought he had come across footprints or something instead of the real thing. They were near the bottom of a wide gulley, nosing about among *Justicia* shrubs and what the goats had left of dehydrated grass tussocks. One of them was browsing on a small acacia bush. Click-click-click, I took the last pictures of the reel in rapid succession as they moved off up the gulley. They grouped together for a few seconds to look back then bolted once more. The youth was already in position ahead of them and he caused the male to break back and run past me. I carried a second camera already loaded and with it I snapped what I shall always believe was the best shot of all. Through the lens even his horns were clear. I say I shall always believe it to be the best shot but I shall never know, for in Addis I posted the film off to London for processing and that was the last I saw of it.

For the rest of the afternoon we kept watching and stalking but the beira had been frightened and they knew they were being hounded. I couldn't get as close again and in the early evening we left them chinking over the stones, still only a mile or so from where we had first sighted them, and not so very far from where their ancestors, perhaps, were immortalised by Powell-Cotton more than seventy years before.

Epilogue

While this book was being written a small group of military officers was planning the successful *coup d'état* of 1974. The initial stages, at least, of the 'creeping coup' were skilfully carried out. The moves were made with caution but were none the less decisive for that, and popular support was carefully monitored at each step in the takeover of power. The final plunge came when Emperor Haile Selassie himself was made a political prisoner. By that time there was no one left to support him for most of the once-powerful loyalists had already been imprisoned. The Ras Mengasha Seyoum of Tigre was one of the few who escaped; he fled to Eritrea, the secessionist province.

Things became more bloody and reckless later on when the different factions of the military junta fell out among themselves and dozens of the aristocrats and overlords of the old feudal system were withdrawn from prison and summarily shot. Before long thousands of people were dying in an intensified war with the separatists in Eritrea.

So another chapter has been opened in Ethiopia's long and turbulent history and if you have stayed with me thus far you might well wonder what difference it will make to the Ethiopian scene as I have described it. No doubt the political writers will give us a detailed analysis and make their predictions but some things already seem to be pretty certain.

The students in Addis, who for years had been agitating for political change, were paraded in uniform to martial music and dispatched to the provinces to carry their knowledge to the ignorant. It was a worthy task they were given, for only three per cent of Ethiopians are literate, but I doubt if it was quite the role that the socialist rebel students had in mind for themselves. Ethiopia, it appears, is to be led very firmly along a hard-line socialist path.

But things Ethiopian are unlikely to change in a hurry. There is a tremendous inertia. Helmsmen may come and go and all sorts of courses may be plotted, but the ship is too big and has been too long at sea to be thrown about like a canoe. Even a semblance of national unity will be difficult to maintain in a land of such immense diversity. I find it hard to imagine the nomads of Afar and Ogaden or the tribesmen of the west marching about in cloth caps and blue uniforms, and I cannot for the life of me see them in the same parade. I doubt whether anyone else seriously imagines this either.

When the military rulers published their manifesto they were understandably most concerned with grass-roots issues such as land tenure. The feudal system is gone, they claimed, farmers will no longer be the exploited tenants of rich and callous landlords. Private lands will be nationalised and farmers will get a fair deal. The Emperor himself had been particularly concerned about the same problem, though he did not think in terms of nationalisation or communes. Legislation had already been drafted to improve the tenant farmers' lot and give the peasants a better opportunity to acquire land of their own.

'The fruits of the farmer's labour must be enjoyed by him whose toil has produced the crop,' said the Emperor in his throne speech to parliament in 1961. But, not surprisingly, the legislation was never passed, for those responsible for its progress included some of the most exploitive landlords of all.

All this has already changed insofar as the crown lands and other vast estates have been declared public property. Some of these lands include areas which have been proposed for conservation measures and the process of setting aside parks and reserves ought to have been very much simplified. Nevertheless there will still be problems in acquiring land for conservation or any other national purpose. Ownership has first to be determined, often without any documentary evidence, and rights of ownership and special rights to land-use have to be unravelled. Occupants are frequently unwilling to leave ancestral lands (in some provinces more than 90 per cent of owned holdings are inherited) or to move out of tribal areas. There are even instances of special spiritual significance attaching to land; to the Karraiu of Awash, for example, Mount Fantalle is a holy place. Above all there is a desperate shortage of funds with which to meet the costs of acquisition and development.

These are fundamental problems indeed and they may well become more troublesome as time goes by. It is no help that in their manifesto Ethiopia's new rulers made no reference to the most basic problem of all and the root cause of most environmental ills – human numbers.

There is an old story about an imaginary microbe which reproduces by splitting in two every minute. At noon a scientist placed it in ideal breeding conditions in a container and at midnight the container was half full. The question is, when will the container be full? The answer, which seems to surprise a great number of people, is one minute past midnight. If a population doubles in a certain time then it doubles, with profoundly different consequences, whether there is one couple at it or one billion.

In Ethiopia the doubling time is about twenty-eight years for the present rate of increase is around 2·5 per cent a year. In some provinces the under-fifteens already make up nearly half the population. This means that even if people could be compelled to restrict their family size to 'replacement level' the population would continue to grow for decades since it would take that long for the breeding proportion to come into balance with the dying proportion. Actually, we can expect the rate of increase to accelerate as death control in the form of malaria eradication, provision of clinics, medicine and hygiene instruction spreads into the rural areas. By the end of the century, unless catastrophe intervenes, a doubling of present numbers is inevitable. The pressure on land is going to intensify, whatever the political climate, and unless agricultural production keeps pace (on a global scale, despite the green revolution, food production has not kept pace with population growth during the seventies), there will be food shortage as well.

There are those who believe that the conservation of wilderness and wildlife is already a lost cause; that we will pretty soon have no choice about what to do with land. Certainly it is unrealistic to believe that wild, unspoiled places can survive for very much longer without special protection; too much has already gone. Once areas have been made safe it remains to be seen for how long we can hang on to them. It is a state of affairs which depresses some people in the extreme but makes little impression on others and actually pleases the rest. There is an understandable attitude in underdeveloped countries that wild animals and wild country ought to be got rid of. They are primitive conditions, associated with backwardness, and should very properly disappear, like disease, as a nation advances towards 'development'. This idea survives despite the fact that, in the crowded west, national parks have deteriorated through over-use and the demand for outdoor recreation is increasing by about ten per cent every year.

Ethiopia, with its deserts, savannas, dripping forests, high moors, humid valleys, lakes and tropical swamps, is a land of magnificent, almost fabulous variety. Despite temporary political upheavals it is a country which growing numbers of people will wish to visit. The demand for new experiences in travel already exists and Ethiopia has so much to offer which industrial societies have lost. For conservation the circumstances are not at all unfavourable. The ibex of the Simien Mountains, for instance, live not merely in inaccessible mountains but among ancient history and scenery so grand as to be uniquely rewarding to visitors whether they are interested in ibex or not. The mountain nyala and Simien fox occur together with no less than thirteen of Ethiopia's twenty-three endemic birds in a compact area of gladed mountain forest where riding and trekking could be a delight and the trout fishing is first class. In the Rift Valley only a range of rugged hills separates the glorious Lake Shalla from the clamour of Abiata's birds. Swayne's hartebeest gallop in a ready-made game reserve by freshwater lakes which hold the best in African sporting fish. Things could be far less convenient.

The mountains and valleys of Ethiopia will endure and no doubt for years to come the rural scene will continue to look much the same over most of the country. But the burning, ploughing, erosion, shooting and trapping are destroying the remaining pockets of forest and wildlife and unless the destruction can be arrested, and quickly, future journeys through the old Empire will be thoroughly saddening tours.

A few, a precious few, Ethiopians realise all this. They have travelled at home and abroad, have seen what can be done and understand what is needed. The only hope is that the influence of these men will be strong enough in the new Ethiopia.

Index

Abarro, Mount, 54
Abaya, Lake, 54, 55-6, 59, 64
Abiata, Lake, 32, 34-42, 99, 101, 107, 215
Abobo, 122
Abol, 125-6
Abyssinian ground hornbills, 61
Acacia mellifera, 63
Acacia nubica, 100
Addis Ababa, 17, 19-21, 32, 75, 114-15, 130, 183-6
Afar Depression, 24-9, 201, 205. *See also* Danakil Depression
African hawk-eagles, 202
Ahmed Gran, 17
Akobo River, 118
Alemayu, Major, 191-2
Alemo (game-guard), 131-2, 134, 137, 143
Amaro Mountains, 59, 60
Amhara people, 17, 33
Anksha (guide), 134-5, 139, 141, 142-3
antelopes, 26, 60, 138; beira, 198, 200, 204-6, 208-11; dibatag, 190, 192-5, 197; gerenuk, 85-7, 136, 178, 190; kob, 123; kudu, 63-4, 85, 87, 104, 178; lechwe, 123-5; nyala, 46, 54; roan, 128; Soemmering's gazelle, 26, 168, 196, 209
Anuak tribe, 119, 124-5, 129
Arba Minch, 56-7, 58, 69-70, 72-3
Arbore, 101-2
Arroweina, 200-1, 205, 206
Arussi Mountains, 45, 46
Arussi tribe, 33
Assab, 21-3, 24
Awari, 189
Awash National Park, 159, 184-6
Awash River, 184, 185, 186
Axum, 16
Aysha, 201, 204-5

babbler, 129-30
Babile, 189
baboons, 89, 104, 149-50, 165, 184-5, 208
Baco, 76, 80-2, 131, 132, 143
Bale province, 46
Baro River, 117-18, 130
Bati, 27
beira antelope, 198, 200, 204-6, 208-11
beisa oryx, 87, 184
Berhanu (game-guard), 57, 60, 61, 67-8, 69, 72, 119, 120, 122, 123, 125, 127-8, 130
bilharzia, 64
Bio Anot, 205
Blower, John, 18, 32, 49-50, 51-3, 54, 80
Boerhavia repens, 195
Borana, 182
Borrissa, Hussein (game-guard), 160, 161, 162-3, 165-6, 167, 169, 171-7, 179-80, 181
Brown, Leslie, 46, 85, 106, 150, 156
Bulbulla River, 37
Bumé tribe, 89-91; hunting technique, 90-91

bushbuck, 135, 138

Calotropis, 206
camouflage, 208-9
Catha edulis, 187
Chamo, Lake, 54, 56, 59, 64
chat (*Catha edulis*), 187
Chercher Mountains, 186
chika (mud) houses, 36-7, 78
Chiobo, 120, 122
Chiru River, 120
cicadas, 129
Collofu River, 56, 57-8, 70, 71
colobus monkeys, 44, 45, 94, 116, 137
conservation: case for, 31-2, 213-16; national scheme for, 99; for Mago Valley, 138-9
Conso, 99
coral reefs, 22-3
coucals, 137
crocodiles, 64, 68, 70-2, 89; hunting of, 91-3

Dahlac Archipelago, 22
Dallol, 171, 173-5
Dami River, 78
Danakil Depression and Desert, 23, 24-9, 159-81; animal life, 159, 167-9; birdlife, 170, 172; landscape, 24-5, 161-2, 163, 166, 171, 172-3, 175, 178-9; nomads, 25-6; salt caravans, 162-4; salt mine, 170-1; salt works, 172, 175-6; sulphur springs, 175
Danakil people, 25-6, 83, 179-80, 185, 202
Debre Berhan, 30
Debre Marcos, 160
Debre Sina, 29
defassa waterbuck, 60, 122
Degahabur, 189
dehydration, 169-70
Devarik, 147-8, 158
dibatag, 190-5, 197
dikdik, 85, 198
Dire Dawa, 183, 186-7, 188, 201
'Doc' (Montana hunter), 75-6, 79, 80, 88, 94-5
dorcas gazelles, 26, 168
doves, 136, 137
dung beetles, 43

Ein Alla River, 164-7
elephants, 189
Elmenteita, Lake, 106
Ensete (false bananas), 115
Erta Ale crater, 25
eucalyptus, 115
Euphorbia piscidermis, 198

Fafan River, 189, 196
Fantalle, Mount, 184, 214
Fasil, King, 145
Fauna Preservation Society, 183
Fiké, Mount, 42, 48
flamingoes, 35, 36, 37, 38, 106
'Flamingo Feathers' (game-guard), 36, 42, 45, 51, 100-1, 108, 109, 110, 112, 113, 132, 134, 137
foxes, 150, 154, 215
From the Roof of Africa (Nicol), 144n

Galadi, 192, 193-4
Galla people, 17, 55, 185, 196; appearance, 33; gravestone, 45; huts, 37
Gambella, 114, 118-19, 121-30
gazelles, 26, 59, 87, 105, 138, 168, 169, 196, 209
Geech, 151-3
gelada baboons, 149-50
Gemu Gofa, 201
gerenuk, 85-7, 136, 178, 190
Gibbe River, 115
Gilbert, Mike, 183-99

Gilo River, 118, 120, 122, 123-6
giraffe, 86, 136
go-away bird, 197
God's Bridge, 56, 59, 66
Godé, 183, 199
Gog, 122, 126
Gondar, 145-7, 156
Goré, 116, 130
Grant's gazelle, 59, 87, 105, 138
grass-burning, 117-18, 121, 125
greater kudu, 63-4
Grevy's zebras, 104-5
Grimwood, Major Ian, 85
Guenther's dikdik, 85
guinea-fowl, 84
Guraghe people, 115

Hagenia tree, 149
Haile Selassie, Emperor, 212, 213
hamadryas baboons, 165, 185, 208
Hammer Koké, 100
Hammer tribe, 90, 91, 111-13
hammerkops, 120
Harrar (city), 187-9
Harrar province, 182, 186, 201
Harshin Meda, 189
hartebeest, 65-6, 87, 90, 93, 136, 215
hawk-eagles, 202
Hoddo, 96
Horacallo River, 34, 37
hornbills, 61, 116, 197
hyaenas, 43

ibex, 150-1, 155-6, 215
Igezu (game-guard), 100, 108, 109, 112
Illubabor, 115, 116
injera (teff batter), 28
Issa tribe, 181, 202

Jade Sea, 89
Jessen, B. H., 124
Jigjiga, 189
Jimma, 115
Julietta, Lake, 178

Kaffa, 115, 116
Kalam, 96
Karo tribe, 142
Karraiu people, 185, 214
Kebre Dahar, 195, 196, 199
Kelafo, 198
Kembolcha, 28-9
Kerre, 88, 89, 91
klipspringer, 47, 104
kob, 123
Korahe, 196
kudu, 63-4, 85, 87, 104, 178

Lalibella, King, 17
lammergeyer, 152-3
land tenure, 144, 213
Langano, Lake, 32, 34, 49
lechwe, 123-5
leopards, 44, 146
lesser kudu, 85, 87, 178
lions, 101, 146
locusts, 203-4
Logia, 180-1
'Loony, The' (game-guard), 36
Luthy, Karl, 124

Mackay, Roger, 75-80, 88
Mago Valley, 91, 92-3, 135-43; safari to, 131-5; scope for protection, 138-9; variety of game, 135-8
Makelle, 161, 163
marabou storks, 35, 106
Marmar Mountains, 205
'Marrile' warriors, 111-13
Masenga tribe, 122
Maydon, H. C., 150
Mazi River, 78
Menelik II, 17, 104, 115, 182
Mengasha Seyoum, Ras, 159, 212
Miesso, 186

Mitiku, Ato, 204
mole-rats, 194
monkeys, 44, 45, 94, 116, 137
Murlé, 87, 90, 93, 95
Mursé hills, 135, 140
Mursé tribe, 140
Mustayel, 188, 198

Nachisar plains, 59-73; animal life, 63, 65-6, 70-2; insect life, 61-3; lakes, 59, 64-5, 67
nagana, 140
National Parks, 31; Awash, 159, 184-6; Omo River area as, 84-5; Rift Valley need for, 46; Simien Mountains, 144-5, 149-58
Neri River, 135, 137-9, 141
Nicol, Clive, 144n, 149
nightjars, 128
Nile lechwe, 123
Nuer tribe, 119, 124
nyala, 46, 54

Ogaden, 182-3, 189-99, 200; animal life, 190, 192-4; birdlife, 197; vegetation, 190, 193, 195-6, 198
olive baboons, 89, 104, 184-5
Omo River, 75, 76, 78, 82, 84-5, 97-8, 115, 135, 141-2
oryx, 87, 105, 138
ostriches, 26-7, 87, 170

pelicans, 35, 47-8
Philip (game-guard), 118, 120, 121, 122, 123, 124, 125, 126, 127
'Plain of Death', 135, 140
plant plankton, turnover rate, 38-9
plovers, 165
Powell-Cotton, P. H. C., 200, 201, 204, 205, 210, 211

Ras Dashan, 153
ravens, 55
reedbuck, 60, 122, 138
Rift Valley, 24, 32, 215; birdlife, 34-5, 37-8, 47-9; cattle overstocking, 34; forest, 44-6; lakes, 32, 34-7, 38-42, 46-9; need for National Park status, 46
roan antelope, 128
Rudolf, Lake, 95

Sagan River, 101, 109, 113
salt-run, 162-4
saltworks, 170-1, 175-6
sand-grouse, 34, 172
Sandhurst Royal Military Academy, 54, 56
Sankaber, 149, 151
secretary bird, 61
Sermale River, 60
Shalla, Lake, 32, 42-5, 46-53, 215
Shalla forest, 44-5, 50
Shashamanne, 54
Shilavo, 197
Shoa province, 17
Sidama people, 55
Sidamo province, 60
Simien Mountains National Park, 144; animal life, 149-51, 154, 155-6; birdlife, 152-3; establishment of, 144-5; Oligocene lava formations, 152
Simon, Noel, 65n
sleeping sickness, 140
Soddu, 55, 98
Soemmering's gazelle, 26, 168, 196, 209
soil conservation, 99
soké boats, 55-6
solifugae, 102-3, 177
Somali wild asses, 159, 167-8
Sporting Trip through Abyssinia, A (Powell-Cotton), 201n, 205
spotted sand-grouse, 172
standard-winged nightjars, 128
Stefanie, Lake, 95, 97, 99-113,

Stefanie, Lake, (*cont'd.*)
170; animal life, 102-3, 104-5, 107; birdlife, 106; vegetation, 103-4, 105
storks, 35, 106
sulphur springs, 175
Swayne's hartebeest, 65-6, 93, 215

Tadessa (Amhara assistant), 76, 78, 82, 83, 88, 89, 90, 94, 95, 96, 98
Tata, Lake, 124
termite mounds, 95
tiang, 87, 90, 107, 128
ticks, 61-3
Tigre province, 16, 159-78
Tribulus, 195
trypanosomiasis, 140
tsetse flies, 117, 134, 140-1
tukul houses, 37, 55, 125, 149
Turmé, 82, 83-4, 95

vervet monkey, 94
vultures, 27, 93, 152-3

Waito River, 101, 109
walia ibex, 150-1, 155-6
warthogs, 178
waterbuck, 60, 122, 123, 138
Werder, 190-2, 195
white-eared kob, 123
wild asses, 159, 167-8
Wildlife Conservation Department, 18, 34, 49, 57, 118, 184
Wollo province, 17, 178-81
wott (stew), 28

Zagwe kingdom, 17
zebras, 63, 104-5
zorilla, 43
Zuquala, Mount, 33
Zawi, Lake, 32, 34, 37